Silver Burdett Picture Histories

The Rise of Islam

Mokhtar Moktefi
Illustrations by Sedat Tosun
English translation by Nan Buranelli

Library of Congress Cataloging-in-Publication Data

Moktefi, Mokhtar.
The rise of Islam.

(Silver Burdett picture histories)
Rev. translation of: Aux premiers siècles d'Islam.
Includes index.
1. Islamic Empire—Juvenile literature. 2. Civilization, Islamic—Juvenile literature. I. Tosun, Sedat. II. Buranelli, Nan, 1917- III. Title.
IV. Series.
DS38.3.M6413 1987 909'.097671 86-11859
ISBN 0-382-09275-9 (lib. bdg.)
ISBN 0-382-09276-7 (soft)

Impreso por:
Edime Org. Gráfica, S. A.
Móstoles (Madrid)

Encuaderna: Larmor, S. A.
Móstoles (Madrid)

I.S.B.N.: 84-599-1832-7 (cartoné)
I.S.B.N.: 84-599-1833-5 (rústica)
Depósito legal: M. 41.268-1986

Impreso en España
Printed in Spain

Translated and adapted for Silver Burdett Press by Nan Buranelli from *La Vie privée des Hommes: Aux premiers siècles de l'Islam.*
First published in France in 1985 by Hachette, Paris.

Adapted and published in the United States by Silver Burdett Press.

Contents

The First Centuries of Islam

INTRODUCTION

We are in Arabia at the beginning of the seventh century of the Christian Era. A single event is about to transform the whole history of the known world — a world dominated by the Persian and Byzantine empires. This momentous event is the birth of Islam, a new monotheistic religion that swiftly acquires millions of believers. But before we examine the event itself, let us take a look at the setting within which Islam grew.

The Arabian Peninsula is a huge region consisting mostly of desert. It is about 1.2 million square miles, or nearly one-half the size of the United States. The landscape varies widely. Some areas are vast stretches of sandy dunes, such as the Nafud in the north and the Rub al-Khali (the "Empty Quarter") in the southeast. Other areas are covered with black volcanic rocks. Still others have vegetation like that of the steppes or savannas — a terrain that in places permits the development of agriculture. Across the Arabian Peninsula there are many oases, where date palms, in particular, grow. The temperature is very hot everywhere. It is the almost complete dryness that has transformed the greater part of the land into a desert.

Roger-Viollet

Aeration and service wells of a *qanat*, an underground system of canals.

Only Yemen and Asir in the south, where there are high mountains, and Oman in the east receive enough rain from the monsoons to permit agriculture to be pursued regularly. In these areas, cultivation of the soil has flourished since antiquity, thanks to a good irrigation system and the use of terrace farming making more land suitable for cultivation. On the southern coast of the peninsula, tropical vegetation — particularly trees bearing myrrh and resin for incense, two sources of the wealth of olden times — flourishes.

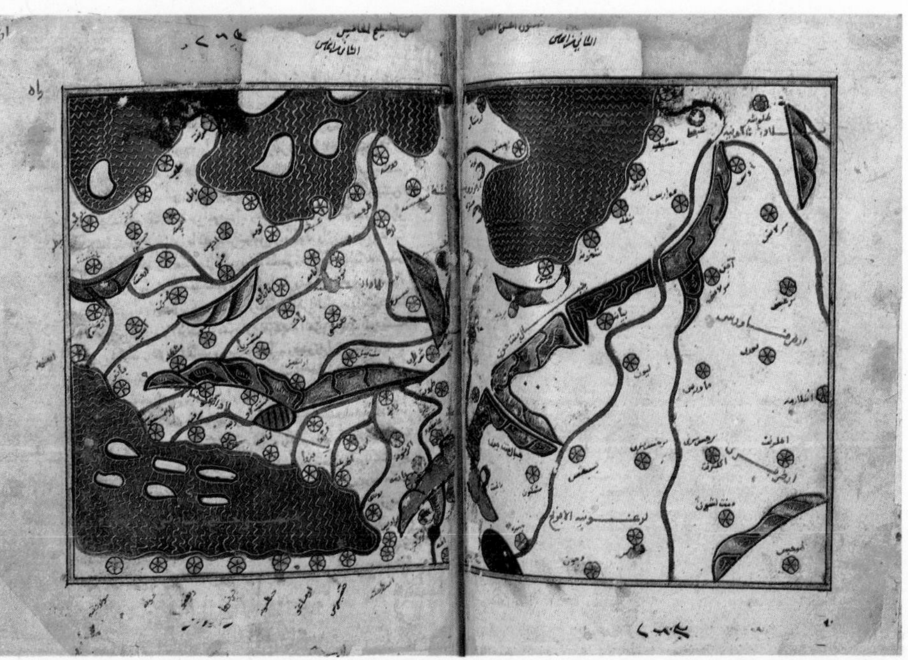

B.-N. Estampes, Paris.

A map from an atlas made by the Arab cartographer al-Idrisi in 1154 for King Roger II of Sicily. Al-Idrisi constructed a silver map of the world which measured over twelve feet in diameter.

THE ARABS BEFORE ISLAM

At a time when Europe was living through the end of the Ice Age, Arabia was enjoying a more temperate climate. Today's deserts were once covered by savannas and pastureland. In the Quaternary geological period, the inhabitants were hunters and used tools hewn from stone. Many sepulchral mounds containing burial chambers date from the third millenium B.C. Recent digs have yielded important archaeological discoveries; they show that at the beginning of the second millenium B.C. close ties existed between the eastern coast of Arabia and the Indus Valley. Coastal towns, like towns in the valley, were built according to a circular, geometric plan.

The Arabs were known to the Egyptians from earliest antiquity. As early as the ninth century B.C., texts mentioned Arabs populating the northwestern part of the peninsula, the deserts of Syria and Mesopotamia, and various states in the south.

The Arab peoples founded many kingdoms, among them the Nabatean, with its spectacular capital, Petra, south of the Dead Sea, and the empire of Palmyra, in the Syrian desert. Both existed at the same time as the Roman Empire and owed their wealth to the caravan trade.

Between the fourth and sixth centuries of the Christian Era, two great Arab states were founded: one in Mesopotamia and Syria, the other in Transjordan. The first, founded by the Lakhmid family, was allied in the beginning with the Romans and then later with the Iranian Sassanids (the Persians). This state protected the Christians.

The second Arab state was ruled by the Ghassanid family, who converted to Christianity and entered the service of the Byzantines. The confrontations between the two states, supported by the two great rival powers, the Persians and the Byzantines, made these two Arab states famous.

In A.D. 510 in southern Arabia, a sovereign adopted Judaism and persecuted the Christians. Ethiopia, encouraged by Byzantium, intervened and put into power a southern Arabian nobleman faithful to Ethiopia. Then in 575, Persia seized Yemen.

The importance of southern Arabia sprang from its economic role. The region produced spices and aromatics, very precious commodities in the commerce of antiquity. In addition, its geographic location made this region the crossroads of commerce between the Far East and both Africa on the one hand, and the countries around the Mediterranean on the other. These riches encouraged the creation of a state with rules and laws, as well as the organization of a very elaborate society. Many traces of these kingdoms of the south have been uncovered by archaeologists: rich and prosperous towns, sumptuous temples, solid walls and towers, hydraulic installations, and numerous art objects including statues, masks, and steles showing scenes of daily life.

A very different way of life reigned in the rest of the peninsula. The nomadic way of life, a result of the natural conditions, had for a very long time been the way of life of the majority of the population of central Arabia. The Bedouin clans followed their livestock, their assurance of survival. In the rainy season, certain desert regions were covered with green vegetation.

When the rainy season ended, the Bedouins would split up into small groups and lead their flocks in search of pasture, moving from one water hole to another. Farmers have settled at the oases and cohabited with the Bedouins since the beginning of time. Both groups exchanged the products of their respective labors.

Before the birth of Islam, the southern Arabs worshiped many gods and goddesses. These divinities were the objects of a cult in temples where powerful priests watched over the riches offered to the gods by the people.

The northern Arabs believed in spirits, or *djinns.* Each tribe had its own divinities. Numerous sanctuaries were scattered across the desert; the most important of these were places of pilgrimage. Sacred enclosures surrounded them

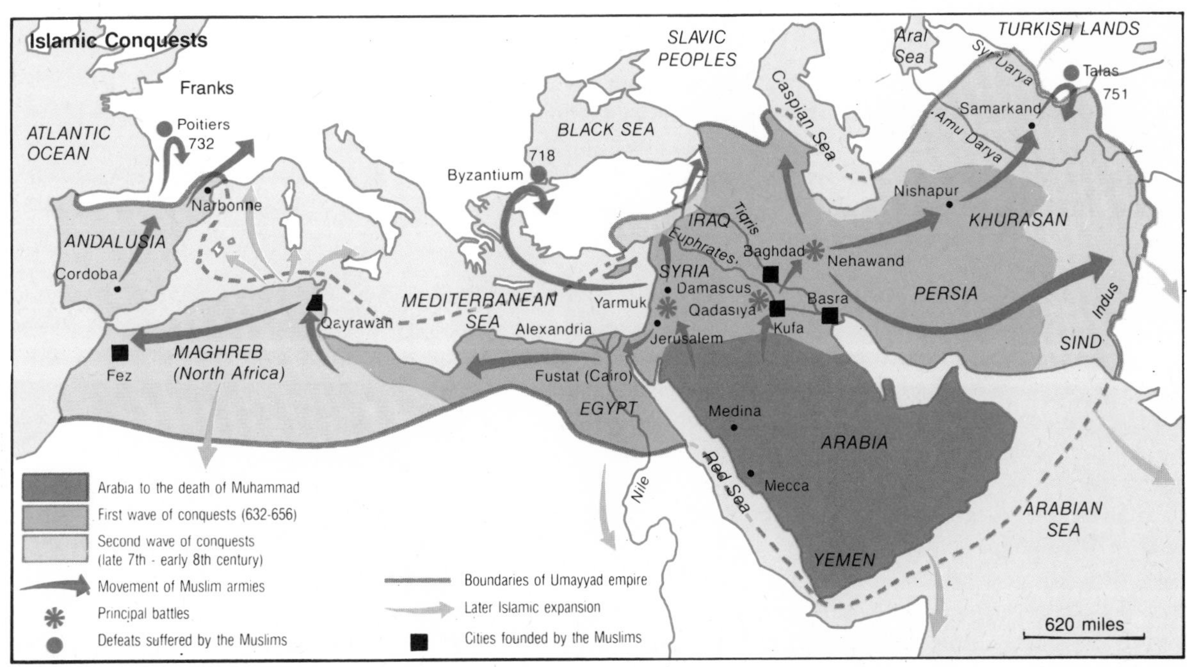

Paul Almasy

The construction of bridges helped to develop the caravan trade.

and provided asylum for those who took refuge in them. In this society, soothsayers and magicians were to be met everywhere.

Beyond the Arabian Peninsula at the time of the birth of Islam, two great powers shared the known world. The first was the Byzantine Empire, with its capital Constantinople (modern-day Istanbul). The "new Rome" in the service of Christianity, this empire considered itself the center of the world. The second, the empire of the Sassanid Persians, stretched from Mesopotamia to the Persian Gulf. The Byzantine Empire and the Persian Empire were in constant confrontation. Each tried to dominate the other and to control the great trade routes to Africa and the Orient, the source of precious cargoes of silk, ivory, and spices. Because of its towns, its southern ports, and its Bedouin caravans, Arabia played an important part in this rivalry. Since neither of the two empires was able to conquer Arabia, each tried to have allies in it.

In the end, southern Arabia suffered the injurious consequences of these many struggles and grew weak, while the Bedouins succeeded in dominating the caravan routes. This new situation allowed all of western Arabia to develop economically. The towns grew larger and became important trade centers. Great fairs were organized, and Arabia gradually assumed a new appearance. In the sixth century the fair of Mecca (*Makka* in Arabic) became one of the most important. Situated on the caravan route between Syria and Yemen, in the rocky valley of the Hijaz, near a watering hole, and around a famous sanctuary, Mecca prospered.

THE BIRTH OF ISLAM

The aristocracy of Mecca belonged to the tribe of the Quraysh, which was divided into several clans, among them the Hashemites and the Umayyads. The latter had political and military control of the town while the Hashemites were respected for their honesty and uprightness. Muhammad (Mahamot), who, according to tradition, was born about A.D. 570 belonged to the Hashemites. Deprived of a father from birth, he lost his mother at six years of age. Muhammad was then entrusted to his uncle abu-Talib, who taught him to be a caravan leader.

At about the age of twenty-five, Muhammad entered the service of Khadija, a rich widow and caravan owner of Mecca. He later married her. Several children were born of this marriage, but only one, a girl named Fatima, survived. Later, Fatima married Ali, the son of abu-Talib.

Muhammad used to go to meditate in a grotto on Mount Hira near Mecca. It was there that, at the age of forty, he first received the word of God, in the the form of a vision of the angel Jibril (Gabriel).

It was some time before Muhammad was able to convince himself that he was not possessed by the devil. Then in about 613, convinced that he had received a divine revelation and that it was God's will that he transmit the message to everyone, Muhammad began preaching his belief in one God and struggling against the ancient idols. His first converts were Khadija, his wife, and Ali, his cousin, along with some other relatives, young people, and the poor. But in general the reaction, including that of the chief of the Quraysh tribe of Mecca, was skeptical, scornful, and, sometimes, even hostile. The new small community of believers was disturbed. Life in Mecca became difficult, and some of its members decided to emigrate to Ethiopia.

In 622, Muhammad decided that he, too, would leave Mecca. He went to Yathrib, now called Medina (Madinat-an-Nabi, "the city of the Prophet"). The year 622, the date of the Hegira (from *hijra*, meaning "migration"), marks the beginning of the Muslim (or Islamic) Era, and equals year I of the Hegira. (A.H. is an abbreviation for "after the Hegira" just as we write A.D. for the Christian Era.)

At Yathrib, people listened to Muhammad's words, and he soon became a real chief of the state. But he continued to receive the divine revelation, the Koran. He organized his companions and allies into a homogeneous community, united within itself without bond to any clan or tribe. His principles were based on equality and social justice. In 630, after years of exile and of "holy" war (that is, of a constant struggle to spread his faith), Muhammad entered Mecca as its conqueror. The Quraysh and almost all the towns, oases, and tribes of Arabia submitted themselves to the will of *Allah,* the one God, as it was revealed by the Prophet. That is the meaning of the world *Islam,* and one who submits to the will of God is a Muslim. Except for the abolition of the old forms of worship, no reprisals were taken against the Mec-

In 696 a reform stabilized Muslim currency. It was based on two legal coins issued by the state: the gold *dinar* and the silver *dirham.* Small coins of bronze and copper, called *fulus* were used for smaller values.

The town of Qayrawan and its great mosque were founded by Uqba ibn-Nafi in 670. But the present minaret dates only from the ninth century.

cans, the inhabitants of the city. After a last visit to his native city, known as the "pilgrimage of farewell," Muhammad died on June 8, 632, without leaving a male heir.

THE "HEIRS" OF THE PROPHET

Muhammad did not name a successor. After his death, his principal companions decided to elect a caliph (the Prophet's lieutenant) to be head of the Muslim community. The first four caliphs — abu-Bakr (632–634), Umar (634–644), Uthman (644–656) and Ali 656–661) — directed the expansion of Islam.

Abu-Bakr, the first caliph, managed to consolidate the hold of Islam over the Syrian tribes. With Umar, Islam spread simultaneously into Asia (Mesopotamia, Syria, Persia, Palestine, Armenia) and Africa (Egypt and Libya). Until then, the Koran — the word of God — had been transmitted orally. Thanks to Uthman, the third caliph, it was written down. For this task, the caliph got the Prophet's chief companions to work together. The sacred text had 6,236 verses divided into 114 chapters and classified in order of decreasing length. The present, official edition of the Koran is the result of these labors.

The Umayyad Caliphate In the new territories, control over the local governors by the caliphs proved difficult. The division of booty and, in particular, of taxes between the provinces and the central government posed serious problems for the caliphs. Some governors were removed; others worried about being removed.

Rumbles of discontent soon led to a conspiracy. In June, 656, Uthman was assassinated. In the midst of the confusion, Ali — cousin of the Prophet and husband of Fatima, the Prophet's daughter — was proclaimed caliph. Unlike his predecessors, Ali was not acknowledged by everyone. Partisans of the murdered caliph, determined to avenge him, united behind Mu'awiya, governor of Syria and a relative of the dead man. This was the first *fitna,* or rupture in the community — the first schism in Islam. In 657 the battle between Ali's troops and Mu'awiya's troops took place at Siffin on the Euphrates, a place situated between Syria and Mesopota-

Rapho/Bright

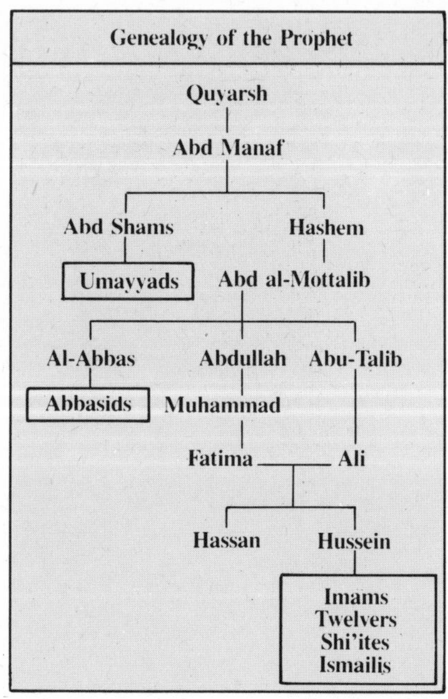

The Mosque-University al-Azhar ("The Splendid") in Cairo. Begun in 972, it is still an important center of Islamic education today.

mia. Some of the Prophet's companions refused to engage in a fratricidal struggle. After several days of fighting, Mu'awiya's soldiers, hard pressed, raised pages from the Koran on the tips of their lances and asked for the kind of arbitration recommended by the sacred writings. Ali agreed.

The arbitration of January, 658 consisted of deciding what in Uthman's behavior could justify his assassination. Six months later the representatives of the two camps agreed on his innocence. When the news was announced, Mu'awiya's supporters believed that the verdict put the blame on Ali, who had refused to condemn the assassins, and they immediately proclaimed their own chief to be the caliph. In an agreement with Mu'awiya, Ali kept Iraq. But his supporters, the Shi'ites, who backed him as a member of the Prophet's family, would never accept his removal. Three years after the arbitration, Ali himself was assassinated. Mu'awiya and his descendants created the Umayyad dynasty (661–750), named after their ancestor Umayya. The first four caliphs had been elected. In the future the caliphate would be inherited, that is, the caliph would be succeeded by his son. Syria and its capital, Damascus, became the center of the new empire that the Umayyad dynasty would rule during the ninety years of its existence.

THE EXPANSION OF ISLAM AND THE BIRTH OF THE MUSLIM WORLD

The Persian Empire had already crumbled before Islam was introduced. Byzantium also was on the decline by 600 A.D. All of North Africa, called the Maghreb by the Arabs, was conquered between 670 and 700. Fifteen years later, the Muslims were attacking Europe; they seized Spain, crossed the Pyrenees into France, then crossed the Garonne River and came within sight of the Loire River between Tours and Poitiers, there the Muslims were defeated by the Franks in 732. During the same period, the Muslim advance to the east carried their armies to Chinese Turkestan, while the new Islamic navy penetrated the Bosporus Strait and laid unsuccessful siege to Constantinople several times.

Accompanying this rapid expansion was the establishment of Muslim authority by means of an administrative organization at once unique and centralized. Soon the Arabic language replaced Greek and Persian in the administration of the conquered lands. A common currency with inscriptions in Arabic circulated throughout the empire. It consisted of two coins: the *dinar,* the monetary unit of gold, and the *dirham,* that of silver. As the frontiers of the empire stabilized, the treasury came up against an unexpected difficulty in collecting its money. The newly converted populations wished to benefit from the same fiscal rules as the

Rapho/R. Michaud

The imposing minaret Qutb Minar in Delhi, India, was built around 1192.

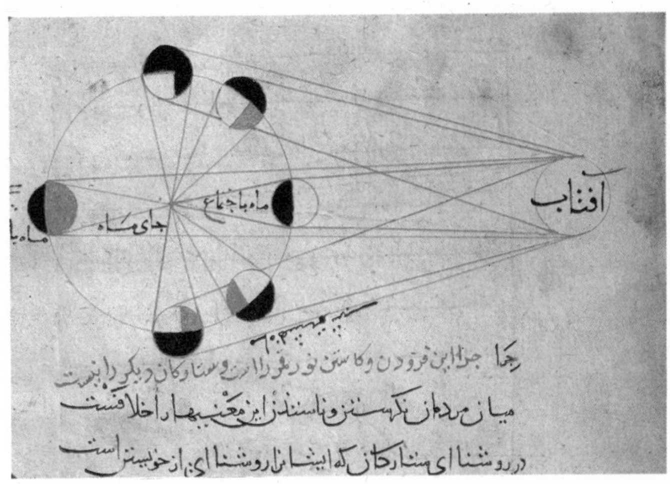

Rapho/R. Michaud

This diagram shows the eclipses of the moon. The diagram is taken from a manuscript of the great scholar and writer al-Biruni.

Muslims. When the authorities refused, the farmers gradually left the countryside for the towns, where they encountered increased insecurity and disorder.

The Abbasid Caliphate In the meantime, to the East, the Shi'ites and Alids, partisans of Ali (son of abu-Talib, the paternal uncle of the Prophet Muhammad), were joined by other "supporters of the family" — those of the second paternal uncle, al-Abbas. Their combined revolutionary propaganda, vigorously conducted from the eastern Iranian province, Khorassan, ignited a civil war and succeeded in overthrowing the power of the Umayyads in less than two

The Great Mosque of Cordova was founded in 785. The prayer room has 1,400 columns topped by horseshoe arches. Hanging from the cedarwood ceiling, 4,700 silver lamps once lighted this sumptuous forest of columns.

Rapho/Pavlovsky

years. The descendants of Abbas, who had only used the help of the Shi'ites for their political ambitions, but were not Shi'ites themselves, established themselves in place of the Umayyads as the Abbasid dynasty which lasted from 750 to 1258. The capital of the empire was moved east to Iraq, to the cities of Kufa and then to Baghdad. The Muslim capital became a brilliant center of world culture, and its influence spread even to the Far East. A considerable number of other towns, trying to imitate the capital, were scattered throughout the empire. They far outshone the tiny cities found in the medieval West of that same period of time.

From the eighth to the ninth century, the Abbasid empire experienced the peak of its power, but it fell to pieces shortly thereafter and gave birth to two new rival caliphates. At the western end of the empire, in Spain, the city of Cordova developed as a dangerous rival. Indeed, a survivor from a massacre of the Umayyad family by an Abbasid general had fled to Spain and succeeded in reestablishing the dynasty there. From the ninth to the eleventh century, Muslim Spain became one of the two centers of world culture. Its capital, Cordova, asserted itself as the most cultivated city in Europe, if not the jewel of the world. The second caliphate was founded by the Shi'ites, who had been betrayed by the Abbasids. One of their factions succeeded in seizing power in North Africa in 910 and proclaiming as caliph Ubayd Allah, who claimed descent from Ali and from Fatima, the Prophet's daughter. This Fatimid dynasty (910–1171) conquered Egypt and in 969 founded Cairo, its new capital. Intellectual and artistic life developed there, in competition with Baghdad.

However, these political and religious conflicts led to a weakening of the central caliphate and to the flourishing of local autonomous powers. About 1050, at the two ends of the Muslim world, two similar reactions took place. Turkish nomads called Seljuks, (recent converts to Islam who were named after Seljuk, the first of them to accept Islam), invaded the eastern regions and created for themselves an empire stretching from Tashkent in Central Asia to Mecca. In the west the Berbers (nomads from the western Sahara who also were newly converted to Islam) established the Almoravid dynasty in North Africa and Spain between 1056 and 1147. This in turn was overthrown by the dynasty of the Almohads (1130–1269). These nomads became sedentary, adding some of their own customs to the urban civilization they conquered.

As we have just seen, the Muslim civilization was born and knew its golden age during the five centuries that correspond to the Christian or Western Middle Ages. Obviously, the history of Muslim civilization did not end in the thirteenth century A.D. It constitutes the common trunk, the point of reference, for today's one billion Muslims. So to understand better the world we live in, as well as for the pleasure of rediscovering the past, let us go back more than thirteen centuries. . . .

Cupola above the mihrab (the prayer niche, indicating the direction to Mecca) of the Great Mosque of Cordova (Spain).

Rapho/Paolo Koch

Chronology

C. 570: Birth of Muhammad in Mecca.

622: Hegira, or migration of Muhammad to Yathrib (Medina), year 1 of the Muslim calendar.

632: Pilgrimage of Muhammad to Mecca.

632: Death of Muhammad in Medina on June 8.

THE FIRST CALIPHS

632–634: Caliphate of Abu Bakr.

634–644: Caliphate of Umar. Conquest of Syria, Iraq, Upper Mesopotamia, Armenia, Persia, Egypt, and Cyrenaica. Foundation of the cities of Basra, Kufa, and Fustat.

644–656: Caliphate of Uthman. Establishment of the official text of the Koran.

656: Assassination of Uthman on June 17.

656–661: Caliphate of Ali.

657: Battle of Siffin, between the partisans of Ali and Mu'awiya, governor of Syria.

661–750: THE UMAYYADS

661–680: Caliphate of Mu'awiya I. Beginning of the Umayyad dynasty.

670: Foundation of the Great Mosque of Qayrawan. Qayrawan made capital of North Africa.

673–677: The Arabs besiege Constantinople.

680–683: Caliphate of Yazid.

680: Husayn, son of Ali and grandson of the Prophet, is killed in a military clash on October 10. The Shi'ites hold Yazid responsible for his death.

710: Construction of the Great Mosque in Damascus.

711: The Muslims invade the Indus Valley and the Iberian peninsula.

732: The Arabs are defeated at the battle of Poitiers in France.

740: The Muslims reach the coast of East Africa.

750–1258: THE ABBASIDS

740–754: Al-Saffah, first Abbasid caliph.

751: The Muslims defeat the Chinese in Central Asia.

756: Establishment of the Umayyad Emirate in Cordova, Spain.

762: Foundation of Baghdad as the new capital.

778: Charlemagne's forces defeated at Roncevalles.

786–809: Caliph Harun al-Rashid.

831: The Arabs capture Palermo, Sicily.

875: Massacre of Muslim merchants in China.

910: The Shi'ites (partisans of Ali) capture Qayrawan, Tunisia. Establishment of the Fatimid dynasty (910–1171).

922: The Bulgars of the Volga region convert to Islam.

969: Cairo becomes the capital of the Fatimid dynasty.

1050: The Banu-Hilal Arabs reach the Maghreb.

1055: The Seljuk Turks capture Baghdad.

1060: The Normans take Sicily from the Arabs.

1062–1147: The Almoravid dynasty established in West Africa and Spain.

1099: The Crusaders capture Jerusalem.

1147–1269: Establishment of the Almohad dynasty in North Africa and Spain.

1187: Salah el-Din (Saladin) recaptures Jerusalem.

1258: The Mongols capture Baghdad, ending Abbasid rule.

At the Dawn of Islam: Mecca Becomes a Crossroads of Commerce

At the northern exit of the city, excitement has reached a peak. The traders' caravan is preparing to leave. The porters and slaves, sometimes helped by the drivers, are securing the last loads on the camels. There are hundreds of one-humped camels (dromedaries), often called "ships of the desert." Each can carry a load of over 200 pounds and is capable of covering at least thirty miles a day. The camel has a legendary reputation for its ability to go long periods without drinking.

By domesticating the camel sometime in the eighteenth century B.C., the Bedouins, the nomads of Arabia, were able to exist more easily in their hostile environment. They ate camel meat, drank camels' milk, and used camel skin and hair to fashion their clothes, their tents, their sacks, and their saddlebags. Camels' dried-up dung was used as fuel for fires in countries where wood has always been scarce. Until the middle of the twentieth century A.D., the raising of camels was an important Bedouin industry.

The caravan preparing to leave has been organized by the city's merchants. The goods from their storehouses have come from distant countries — the Far East, southern Arabia, Ethiopia, East Africa, Egypt, and other Mediterranean lands. The goods are destined for Syria, Palestine, and Mesopotamia. Ivory and gold are there, along with cereals, oils, incense, aromatics, arms, and fabrics. To guarantee the security of the caravan, the camel drivers, who are also excellent warriors, carry arms. The drivers wield daggers, sabers, lances, and bows and arrows. However, the city authorities have also negotiated agreements with the chiefs of tribes controlling the territories the caravan will cross. Safe-conducts (resembling passports) are handed out to the drivers in charge of the caravan.

A camel driver is tying a water-skin and the ivory tusks of an elephant firmly on the back of his beast. A trader is bargaining with the leader of the caravan, asking him to accept merchandise carried by the trader's donkeys. Mecca can be seen in the background.

To make butter the Bedouins churned milk in tanned sheepskins which were hung from tripods. This was usually women's work. In each tent lived one family. A group of families made up a clan, and several clans made a tribe. The heads of the large families elected the *sayyid*, or sheikh, who served as chief of the tribe. The women worked very hard but had relative independence. In certain circumstances a woman could send her husband away. She did so by changing the direction of the tent's entrance.

Markets were held once a week in villages situated on the edge of the desert and in the oases. Important fairs took place each year at the way stations and in the few towns that were on the routes of the great caravan trade.

The Bedouins measured their wealth, their power, and even their degree of nobility by the size of their camel herds. At the market, transactions were always concluded by a vigorous handshake.

The *ghazwa* or *razzia*, a surprise raid to seize the herds of a rival clan, was one of the customs of pre-Islamic Arabia. The raids had to be carried out without anyone being killed. If there was a murder, the law demanded the execution of the murderer or a member of his family.

A Single God, A New Empire

When the Prophet Muhammad died in 632, a huge empire and a great civilization were just coming to life. This one man had set in motion a universal revolution that was soon brought to a large portion of the world. In fact, the Arabs (now Muslims), mobilized behind the caliph, the Prophet's successor, to carry the new divine message to all humanity.

At this time, two great empires shared the known world: the Persian Empire and the Byzantine Empire. The Muslim horsemen and camel drivers, although they were in the minority, managed in ten years to conquer Egypt and Cyrenaica (Libya) in the west, while in the east they routed the Persian emperor's powerful army, which used elephants. One century after the death of Muhammad, Islam and the Muslims reached as far as Poitiers, France, in the western world. In the East they penetrated into Chinese Turkestan. These conquerors were sometimes welcomed as liberators by populations already under the yoke of another foreign power. To the divided and quarreling Christians — and to the mystery of the Trinity, where God is at once Father, Son, and Holy Spirit — Islam brought an answer everyone could understand: God is unique, He has neither father nor son. Muhammad is simply a man chosen by God to carry His Word to the world.

Since the Koran recognizes the Bible as a holy book and considers Abraham, Moses, and Jesus, in particular, as prophets, the Muslims called the Christians and the Jews "People of the Book." They had the status of a protected minority — that is, they were allowed to keep their property, places of worship, and forms of justice, and they had their own representatives with the new authority. In return, the Christians and Jews had to pay a tax while the Muslims did not.

These cavalry fighters are Arab volunteers. The banner fluttering in the wind proclaims that God is one and that Muhammad is his messenger. The cavalry is armed basically with lances, shields, and coats of mail. The flag-bearers wear leather breastplates decorated with copper buttons.

The locations of the camps were chosen for their military importance and to facilitate communications with Medina and, later, Damascus, the first capitals of the empire. Beside the camps, new towns grew up. In particular, Basra and Kufa in Iraq were built in this way, as were Fustat in Egypt and Qayrawan in North Africa. In these centers, the mosque was of primary importance. It was the symbol of Islamic unity. There the believers could gather on Fridays for the communal prayer. Its tower, called a minaret, became a landmark of the Muslim territories.

Fruit and vegetable markets established themselves in the middle of the these new centers, not far from the mosque. Later they would be moved back toward the city's exit. The peasants could display their produce more easily there and, of even greater importance, traffic jams could be avoided.

To ensure the distribution of the Koran, copyists at the mosque busied themselves reproducing it. The text was put in writing shortly after the death of the Prophet Muhammad, under the direction of his first companions. Since then, its contents have remained unchanged.

Within the confines of the mosque, an elderly scholar with his back to a pillar is teaching from the Koran to a group of the faithful as they wait for the hour of prayer. As he reads the text, he explains the historical circumstances of its revelation and makes a religious, moral, social, or political commentary on it.

The Five Pillars of Islam

"I bear witness that there is no other god but Allah, and Muhammad is his messenger." This profession of faith is *shahadah*, the first of the "five pillars of Islam." Whoever pronounces it, with the index finger of their right hand pointed to the sky, becomes a Muslim. Every evening before going to sleep, as though it were the last moment of life, the believer must repeat this witness.

"Allahu Akbar" "God is great..." These words begin the call to prayer. The second pillar of Islam (*salat*) is to pray five times a day. Muslims can pray alone or in a group. However, all the faithful must assemble at the mosque on Fridays at noon. Together they hear the recitation of the Koran, followed by a sermon delivered from a raised pulpit called a *minbar*. Then they begin to pray, standing behind the *imam* (prayer leader) who faces the *mihrab*, an empty niche hollowed in the wall and pointing in the direction of Mecca.

In practicing their faith, Muslims communicate freely with God, without any middleman. Islam has no clergy, or pope.

The third pillar, or duty, is the *zakat*, the giving of alms to the needy. In effect, this is a tax that creates a fund for mutual aid, for solidarity, and for the public interest. A fast during the month of Ramadan is the fourth pillar *(sawm)*. From sunrise to sunset, every adult Muslim in good health abstains from drinking, eating, smoking, and having sexual relations.

Pilgrimage to Mecca *(hajj)* is the fifth and last pillar. All Muslims aspire to make this pilgrimage once during their lives. At the same moment and in the same place, thousands of the faithful of different races and situations gather together wearing the same garment, the *ihram*. They perform together the same gestures, rites, and prayers. There, too, Muslims must remember their duties of justice, tolerance, and love toward other people.

The pilgrims all wear two lengths of the same white cloth. One is wound around the waist; the other is draped over the shoulder. On their feet are leather sandals. The men must shave their heads; the women may keep their hair but must cover it completely. They make seven turns (the first three of them at a rapid pace) around the sacred stone, the *Ka'aba*.

From the top of the minaret, the muezzin *al-mouadhin*, sounds the call to prayer. He does this five times a day. The man who first took on this role in Islam was a freed black slave chosen by the Prophet Muhammad. He was named Bilal.

No one can come to pray without being in a state of purity. In the courtyard of a mosque, this father is showing his son how to perform a ritual ablution before he goes into the prayer room. He must wash his hands, face, and feet. If necessary, sand can be used instead of water.

On their knees, the faithful are finishing their prayers with the *salâm*, or the salute to the Prophet and his community. Muslims begin prayer with the expression "God is great," accompanied by the raising of the hands to shoulder height, and go on to the recitation of the first *sura* (chapter of the Koran) and some verses.

The pastry cooks make fortunes during the evenings of Ramadan. All day long the faithful have controlled their desires. When night comes, they feel the need to celebrate. To some extent, Ramadan celebrates an anniversary. The Koran was beginning to be revealed during this month of the lunar calendar.

At the end of the pilgrimage to Mecca, every wealthy Muslim cuts the throat of an animal, usually a sheep. This gesture is in imitation of Abraham (Ibrahim). According to tradition, God wished to test Abraham by asking him to sacrifice his son. When Abraham prepared to do so, an angel appeared to him — with a sheep as a substitute!

Long-Distance Commerce

The unification of territories that until the advent of Islam had had no contact with other countries, or had been warring with each other, stimulated the spirit of enterprise in the Muslim traders. Long-distance commercial undertakings, both international and interregional and financed either with personal or family capital or with capital raised among partners, sprang up. Trading companies installed representatives in various local markets and sent agents into distant lands.

The highest profits were made by buying low-priced merchandise in one country and selling it for more elsewhere. As in all commercial undertakings, traders had to keep themselves informed to limit their risk. That is why letters and secret messages in code passed between correspondents by the quickest possible routes.

Long-distance trade was nearly always a trade in luxury goods (precious stones, silks, pearls, coral, ivory, furs) and in products like wood, iron, tin, mercury, gold, and silver.

To pay for their transactions, the merchants carried bags of gold and silver coins, but for the most part they used checks and letters of credit. The procedure for these was as follows: The trader would write a letter to a colleague living in another city, asking him to put at the disposal of the bearer of the letter a certain sum for which he, the colleague, would be reimbursed.

A tenth-century chronicler mentioned in his writings the existence of an acknowledgement of debt for a sum of 42,000 dinárs, the equivalent of about 400 pounds of gold. A ship from China or a caravan arriving from the western Sahara would sometimes carry cargoes worth as much as 500,000 dinars!

The Muslim world possessed enough gold to import goods and products from the rest of the known world. The gold dinar reigned supreme over every commercial marketplace, including those on the banks of the Baltic Sea and along the great rivers of Russia.

On the Tigris River, wood from Armenia was floated down to Baghdad. Large rafts carried tree trunks secured with heavy chains. Above each raft rose a mast with a single sail. Although the Muslim world had no great forests, it used vast quantities of wood for its buildings, for its industries, and for cabinetmaking.

In mountainside galleries, miners dug lead containing silver from the great mine at Bendjhir, north of Kabul, in Afghanistan. Important mines could also be found in southern Spain. A special treatment was applied to separate the silver from the lead.

An African market in *Bilad as-Soudan*, "the country of the blacks," welcomed Tuaregs and traders from North Africa. Exchanges were conducted with gold dust and ingots linked together as rings which were traded for salt, dates, copper utensils, and necklaces of glass beads.

Red cinnabar was heated not far from the place where it was mined. It yielded mercury. Mercury is the only metal that is liquid at an ordinary temperature. When it is mixed with the mineral gold and fused with it, the mercury evaporates and leaves behind pure molten gold. This technique is called amalgamation.

Thanks to the mines in Spain, North Africa, Sicily, Iran, and the Farghana in Central Asia, the Muslims had a virtual monopoly on mercury. They also had at their disposal the yield of the largest gold mines in the world.

From China to Spain

From Asia to Europe, in what is called *Dar al-Islam* (the house, or the territory, of Islam), people, goods, and ideas circulated constantly. Traders and shipowners took the place of the warrior-conquerors. Trade routes were organized from Canton in China to Cordova in Andalusia, and from the Caspian Sea to central Africa. Maritime and river ports were developed. Caravan routes with the necessary accommodations were established.

In the ports, towns, and villages, and even on the desert trails, caravanserais welcomed travelers and goods. Usually the caravanserais were enormous fortresses, with single colossal entranceways opening onto vast courtyards. The street levels were taken by the local occupants — the guard-rooms, the stables, and the warehouses for stocking merchandise destined for bulk trade. The upper levels contained the sleeping quarters, bathing facilities, and mosques.

As soon as they arrived, boats and caravans were subjected to customs control. Directed by a supervisor, the customs officers registered the name of the people, their country of origin, a description of them, and a declaration of what was being transported — merchandise and currency. The merchandise was taxed. The zakat, a legal tax, could be collected for sums held for more than a year and exceeding a certain minimum.

Verifications were carried out by examining the cargo. Most of the time the customs officials made their searches courteously. But sometimes they became rude and irritating. Zealous officers had all the bags opened, felt along waistbands, and even asked pilgrims to swear to the truth of their declarations.

Ships like this one, with its great sails, could carry more than a thousand people. It had about a hundred cabins and had a number of shops, including a grocery, a refreshment bar, and a laundry. When the weather was fine and the sea calm, the barber could leave his shop below and set himself up on the deck.

Three princesses have joined a caravan of thousands of pilgrims making their way toward Mecca. The princesses travel in luxurious palanquins carried by camels. Each move of the whole caravan (departures, stops, erecting and dismantling tents) takes place to the sound of drums.

The caravanserais were places for large commercial transactions. Deals were made for all sorts of products and wares from every corner of the world. For payments the traders used letters of credit and *sakk*, or checks.

On the navigable rivers, boats and barks carried merchandise and passengers. Animals were carried on ferries from one bank to the other. In the Baghdad and Basra regions, the townspeople traveled daily on the numerous canals.

The caravanserais were situated on the great caravan routes. Their courtyards usually had pools that served as watering troughs. These way stations were sometimes sumptuous buildings put up by the central government or its provincial agents. Others were erected privately either to encourage trade or, through piety, to help the pilgrims, and were much less luxurious. Sometimes it cost nothing to rest at a caravanserais. In some, food was distributed, or the animals were shod "in the name of a holy man" — that is, for charity's sake.

The Postal and Telegraph Services

From the beginning of the Islamic Empire, the administration of the postal service, the *Diwan al-Barid*, was one of the most important mechanisms of the state. To dispatch the mail under the most favorable conditions, a vast network of relay stations was set up along the most important communications routes throughout Muslim territories. This network consisted of 930 post offices, each two to four *farsakh* or *parasangs* from the next (seven to fourteen miles apart). Fresh mounts awaited the messengers around the clock at these posts, which ranged in size and grandeur from palatial caravanserais to single, roughly constructed buildings.

Faster connections by air were provided by carrier pigeons. The aerial network was very busy because localities not reached by the other postal system were included in this one. As with airmail today, the weight of letters carried by the birds had to be as light as possible — the paper and the size were specially prepared.

Another fast method of communication was used exclusively by the army and was somewhat like a telegraph system. It was a system of sight signaling meant to give the alarm in case of attack or enemy raid along the frontiers of the Muslim Empire. Fire or smoke signals — coded messages, in other words — were sent from the tops of the *ribat* (fortress) towers, from the ramparts of the *barid* (outposts), and from observation posts situated on mountain peaks. In one night a message could cross the 2,100 miles separating Morocco from Egypt.

The director of the postal service and his agents were also responsible for collecting information for the caliphs about the economic, social, and political situations in the provinces.

Military messages were sent by signal lights. From the top of the watchtower of a *ribat* in the Maghreb, a coded message announces to a small fort in the distance the approach of troops. The light from one tower of the fort perched on the hill acknowledges reception of the message.

In registry offices officials would inscribe, in large books, the details of the mail to be dispatched. Payment was collected upon arrival at its destination. All envelopes were sealed by wax. The government, the merchants, and everyone else used seals to stamp their packets. This permitted them to keep their correspondence secret. The engravers of the seals were required to keep records of each imprint and the name of the owner of every seal they made. This shows how much importance was attached to secrecy.

Certain of being easily identified by a scarf (*futa*) of the caliph's colors wrapped around his neck, this cameleer is racing toward the next station. His leather saddlebag is full of urgent mail. An earthenware water bottle and a saber attached to his belt complete his equipment.

Thousands of pigeons wore the insignia of the sovereign on their beaks or claws. They were divided into companies under the command of special officers, and were released from specific areas in the capital's suburbs, or from the terraces and towers, or *barj*, of a *barid's* buildings.

Packets and bulky objects traveled on the backs of mules or camels or in postal service boats along the coasts and on the big rivers. Money in sealed boxes and valuable cargoes were transported under armed guard. The route taken by the postal carriers was not always the same as that of the public caravans. The carriers took the shortest way to their destination, no matter how difficult the terrain. When political or military reasons demanded it, the postal service could be reinforced with more manpower on certain routes.

Soldiers of the Prophet

During the early years of Islam, the horsemen and cameleers coming from Arabia carried only light arms. Their faith, as well as the swiftness of their attack and individual skill gave them power. The conquest of new territory brought an important change. Contingents of men from Syria, the Maghreb, Iran, Africa, and Turkey joined the ranks of their Arab conquerors, who were outnumbered by them. Little by little, the army of volunteers became an army of professionals, and its equipment, like its small arms, improved.

These technicians of war described their trade in treatises giving instruction on laying siege to towns, on tactics, and on strategy. The Turkish and Iranian horsemen, in particular, were experts at aiming their bows and arrows as they rode. They benefited from the protection of the artillery, engineers, and military craftsmen, with their rock-launching siege weapons, crossbows, moving towers and mobile shelters, grenades, and primitive flame-throwers. These incendiary devices and explosives, secret weapons in themselves, alarmed the Crusaders, who described them as "thunder from the sky" or as "flying dragons."

This carefully assembled army was organized, managed, and controlled by the *Diwan al-Jaysh*, or military administration. Sometimes the army enlisted volunteers. The most famous of these were the *murabitun*, the inhabitants of the ribats (forts) that lined the southern Mediterranean coast and certain frontier areas. In the towns, the safety of property and of persons as well as public order were the responsibility of a police corps independent of the army. Although charged with the execution of punishments handed out by the *kadi* (the magistrate), the prefect of police could inflict penalties such as the *bastinado* (striking the soles of the feet) or the whip.

The first line on the banner reads *La Ilaha Illa Allah* and means "There is no god but Allah." The second line reads *Muhammad Rassoul Allah*, which means "Muhammad is the messenger of Allah." This is the motto of the troops who are leaving the town for frontiers menaced by an enemy. The civilians cheer them on and encourage them with prayers.

The tactic used by the Arabs for their first conquests consisted of attacking, pretending to retreat immediately, and then returning suddenly to the battle. This tactic was called *karr wa farr*, "return and flight." Later the Arabs adopted an order of battle with an advance guard, the main force in the middle, two wings, and a rear guard. One of their most effective tricks was to dress cavalrymen and their mounts in felt that had been made fireproof but was soaked in naphtha and then set on fire. The felt protected the men and their mounts as, at night, they were sent hurtling into the enemy camp. Terrified by the flames, the enemy's horses fled, abandoning their riders.

Here are some warriors of the Muslim army. We see, (1) an African foot soldier wearing quilted armor; (2) a member of the imperial guard dressed in a coat of mail; (3) a cavalryman-archer whose horse is protected by a padded covering; (4) a fighting volunteer from a poor tribe; and (5) a member of the light horse cavalry. The light horse served as guards in time of peace and carried out reconnaissance and harassment missions when the army was campaigning.

The navy, like the army, used *naffatoun* — specialists in throwing naphtha, a highly flammable substance. Long, hollowed, and bent tubes, the ancestors of modern flamethrowers, were made into a kind of incendiary siphon. Burning javelins carrying loads of naphtha — sometimes with iron shot — on their tips were also used. In close combat, the enemy was blinded when powerful syringes were used to spray vitriol and other harmful chemicals over them. These chemical weapons also required top-secret research and experiments before they could be employed in battle.

The Bounty of the Countryside

In the Dar al-Islam — that is, in Muslim territory — the rural landscape displayed great diversity. Thus, oases flourished in desert areas, in the midst of vast stretches of sand and rocks. The high plateaus of Iran and North Africa always had very little rainfall. Nomads, herding sheep, roamed these highlands in every direction. In the plains and valleys pierced by great rivers like the Amu Darya, the Tigris, the Euphrates, the Nile, and the Wed al-Kebir (Guadalquivir), a combination of hard work and ingenuity made the country flourish. Even in the mountains, wherever it rained enough, as in Afghanistan, some crops were grown.

From the first century of the Hegira (the Muslim era), villages evolved around the castles of the members of the ruling aristocratic families, especially in Syria. They were close to the court and to the high functionaries of state. Alongside these enormous properties could be found small plots of ground or family holdings, as well as relatively large domains belonging either to local notables or to townspeople.

Sometimes the landowners left the working of their lands to poor peasants or agricultural laborers. Three kinds of contracts governed these arrangements. The most common contract was one in which the worker supplied only physical labor in exchange for a fifth of the crop. The irrigation contract was used for properties with plantations, beasts of burden, and arrangements for distributing water. The farmer worked the land and received half the harvest. The third kind of contract was one in which one party provided the land and the other did the planting. When the land began to yield crops, the worker became proprietor of one share of the cultivated land. This share was fixed in advance.

Seasonal workers, like the ones pictured above, were paid by the day. They harvested the crops using sickles. The wooden rake was used to gather the wheat together before it was tied into sheaves. The sheaves were carried on the backs of donkeys to a threshing area in another part of the field. There a machine drawn by two oxen cut up the straw and crushed the ears. Using wooden forks, others would winnow the grain.

This little village is surrounded by a wall with only one gateway. The village looks like a big farm. In the middle of the courtyard can be seen the fountain-well and, not far from the entrance, the communal oven. The stables occupy the ground floors of the buildings. The granges and the sleeping quarters are above. On the terrace a woman is grinding the grain with a stone hand mill (a quern). In certain areas the villages were composed of cabins or huts made of tightly bound reeds. There, the dwelling was merely a place for shelter.

The rice plantations were situated in warm, marshy areas and on irrigated land. The work of preparation and upkeep of the land required an abundance of labor. When there were not enough farm hands to do the work, children were recruited.

The sled-like machine with cutting wheels was used to thresh wheat, that is, to husk the ears. The machine was pulled by a pair of oxen led by a peasant repeatedly over the threshing area. The wooden cylinders, reinforced by iron disks, chopped the straw and removed the grain from the ears.

At an oil press like the one in the picture, a donkey often turned the enormous mill stone. Elsewhere, camels, buffaloes, or oxen might also be used. Sometimes a hydraulic mill (that is, one moved by water power) was employed to crush the olives before they were sent to the oil press. The press here is being worked by a man. Andalusia, North Africa, and Syria furnished the greater part of the olive oil consumed in the Muslim Empire and even in Byzantium. From this important industry also came soaps and oils destined for factories making essence for perfume.

Advanced Agricultural Technologies

Wherever there was sufficient irrigation, fields stretched for hundreds of acres. Streaked by waterways ranging from small trenches to navigable canals, the flat countryside looked like a magnificent colored embroidery. All kinds of vegetables, except tomatoes and potatoes, were planted. Plants like rice, cotton, eggplant, sugarcane, mulberry trees, lemon and orange trees, and many others, spread along the southern shores of the Mediterranean Sea and into Spain and Sicily. Particularly in Egypt, Syria, and Iran, specialists called agronomists worked to select and improve the varieties of plants. From observation and experimentation, the Muslim agronomists were familiar with the nitrogen-rich leguminous plants, the fruits of which are pods, and with the fertilizers necessary to enrich the earth. They became masters of the art of conserving and distributing water. They rotated the plowing of fields and worked the earth twice to bring air and light to the plants. Books and travelers spread their technology throughout Dar al-Islam.

Hydraulic specialists worked on the techniques of collecting water in basins and diverting it. They perfected water-elevators, which made it possible to raise water to the level of the areas to be irrigated. A corps of state technical experts supervised the digging of great canals and regulated their operation.

A true agricultural revolution, supported by tax reform, resulted in returns that were unbelievable for the period. The Muslims were nine centuries ahead of the physiocrats, the eighteenth-century European economists who believed the land to be the source of all wealth. Muslim scholars and governmental ministers urged the sovereign to consider agriculture, not gold, as the state's principal source of wealth.

By moving around and around, the mule activates the mechanism that allows the main wheel to pull the chain and large buckets. The well is enclosed in a masonry structure. The water empties into a trench and serves to irrigate the crops and gardens. The water-wheel is called a noria, from the Arab *na'ur.*

Nilometers were used to measure the height and land coverage of the Nile floods to calculate the farmers' taxes on the basis of the crop they could hope to gather. A nilometer is basically a well that has been built around a graduated column. This one dates from 715 and is on the island of Roda near Cairo.

Using their imagination and experience farmers obtained new species of fruits and flowers by grafting. The same vine could produce white, black, and red grapes. One tree could bear two different fruits. Roses could be grown with a mixture of white and red petals.

To the techniques of irrigation was added the art of fertilizing the land to produce the best crops. The peasants knew the value of the different natural manures as fertilizers. These people also knew how to prepare fertilizers and how to spread them in the fields.

To irrigate fields that were above the level of the river, a wheel, or noria, was used. But when the waters of a river had to be diverted to distant fields, a canal had to be dug. Hundreds of workers were needed for this task. They were directed by specialized personnel, including engineers, foremen, geometricians, and surveyors. A work of practical mathematics published in the eleventh century showed those responsible for administering the irrigations how to calculate, for example, the amount of work necessary to dig a canal.

Industrial Crops and Impoverished Peasants

The cultivation of land, whether it was dry or irrigated, required a great deal of labor at certain times of year. Small farmers from the same village shared the work with each other. They gathered their flocks together and paid a shepherd to take the flocks to pasture.

An overseer called a *wakil*, had authority over large properties belonging to the sovereign or members of the aristocracy. The overseer made sure that the farming system was running smoothly, relying on foremen on the land and other overseers at the mills and irrigation devices.

The overseer also controlled the tenant farmers and collected the rents. In general, this type of farming consisted of vast plantings for industrial uses, such as sugar cane, cotton, flax, papyrus, and sesame. These crops required a large work force, especially at harvest time. In the area of Sawad in Iraq, the state and its governing body used workers imported from East Africa. The workers were slaves called *zandjs*, who, even though they were Muslims, were systematically exploited in a manner contrary to the precepts of the Koran. In the end they revolted, with support from impoverished peasants and the seasonal farm workers. The revolt disrupted the state's central power for nearly fifteen years.

The fruit tree and banana plantations, the vineyards, the olive groves, the fields of flowers, spices, and tinctorial plants (used for dyeing) yielded products much in demand. These products even came from distant provinces. For instance, raisins came from Palestine and from Malaga in Spain; olives, from Syria and North Africa; figs, from Jerusalem and Iraq; dates, from North African oases and from Iraq; and lemons and grapefruit, from Egypt.

To extract and refine sugar, the stalks were first put into a press, the millstone of which was turned by a man. The extracted liquid was heated in a boiler and reduced by three quarters. Sugar was obtained in the form of syrup, which was then poured into conical clay molds. It stayed in the molds until it solidified.

The revolt of the *zandjs*, black slaves from East Africa, took place in lower Iraq, a land of canals and marshes. Hidden in areas thick with reeds and difficult to penetrate, the zandjs, armed with lances and bows and arrows, terrorized and held the boat traffic on the canals for ransom. Their rebellion, which began in 869, was not crushed until 883. The survivors joined a politico-religious movement called the *Karmats*, which preached social equality. The movement succeeded in forming an independent state in Bahrain and in eastern Arabia.

There were different instruments for carding cotton and wool — that is, for disentangling, separating, and cleaning the fibers. This instrument looked like a kind of archer's bow and was struck with a mallet.

Here a peasant woman is softening the cocoons of silkworms by plunging them into boiling water. Another woman is working a reel to spool the new silk thread. Sericulture, or the breeding of silkworms, and the cocooneries where they were bred extended from the Caspian Sea to Sicily and Spain.

Harvesting cotton began at the very first light of day. Some workers cut open the bolls and filled baskets with cotton. Another worker emptied the basket onto a pile. The cotton was then sorted handful by handful and gathered into little heaps to dry. Then, it was stored. Since these operations were carried out in the open air, the least puff of wind snatched up the lightest wisps. White flakes floated through the whole area. Nothing and no one — not people, animals, or plants — could escape this "snowfall."

The Great Construction Sites

Using their experience and their research, Muslim artisans created buildings that could be regarded as genuine masterpieces. The solutions they found for the complex problems that were presented to them in the areas of public works, architecture, and naval construction — such as those concerning the distribution of water, steam, and smoke in the public baths — turned them into true engineers.

Towns sprang up like mushrooms across the entire Muslim world. Rising out of nothing or built around a small, preexisting nucleus, some towns became huge, brilliant urban centers. At the time that Aachen, the capital of Charlemagne's empire, held fewer than three thousand inhabitants, Qayrawan, Damascus, Samarkand, and many other cities of the Muslim Empire counted their residents in the hundreds of thousands. The population of Cordova is supposed to have reached half a million, and that of Baghdad, around two million.

These were real cities, laid out according to a predetermined plan and with large avenues running in straight lines. In the center stood the principal mosque, the palace of the ruler or of his representative, and the markets. During the building of Baghdad, a city built on a circular plan, the construction yards employed tens of thousands of workers for four years. The masons used bricks, either baked or unfired, or stones. Materials varied according to what could be found in a particular region. For palaces and other important structures, marble, granite, onyx, and rare woods were imported from foreign lands.

Pipes of baked clay or of lead ensured the proper distribution of running water. The water, flowing through canals and aqueducts, was collected in reservoirs and immense cisterns. The ingenious Persian technique known as *qanat* permitted the tapping of subterranean sources and was used in a systematic manner. The same technique spread all the way to North Africa and to Andalusia, which is to say, Muslim Spain.

Workers set marble slabs in place and made them fit by striking them with wooden mallets. Pillars and columns alternated in a regular pattern. The semicircular arch is the most simple curved form. Along with the arcaded gallery two stories high, this arch is characteristic of the Arabic-Muslim architecture of the first century of Islam.

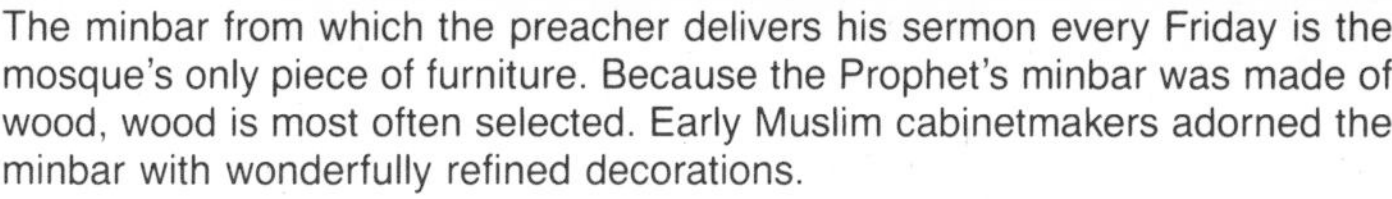

The minbar from which the preacher delivers his sermon every Friday is the mosque's only piece of furniture. Because the Prophet's minbar was made of wood, wood is most often selected. Early Muslim cabinetmakers adorned the minbar with wonderfully refined decorations.

Artists carved in stone, plaster, stucco, and clay. A precise design revealed the art of the sculptor. Pious inscriptions, geometrical forms, and arabesque intertwinings are characteristic of the decorations on monuments from the classical periods of the Arabic-Islamic civilization.

These mosaics are being laid in the pavement of a *hamman* (bath) belonging to a prince. Mosaics were made of glass or colored stone cubes and were laid down according to a detailed pattern. The walls of the Great Mosque of Damascus were made of magnificent panels in mosaics on a gilded background.

The people of the Mediterranean region used pegs to hold the planks of their ships in place. The Orientals assembled the planks alongside the ship and fastened them with coconut fibers; then they filled in the joints and the seams with blubber. Both maritime commerce and war fleets were developed, causing an enormous consumption of wood. Thus, Baghdad had to import wood from Armenia, and Egypt imported teak from India. The trade in wood for shipbuilding was also established with the Christian West.

A Multitude of Artisans

One could spend hours admiring potters at their wheels fashioning by hand, a jug, a vase, a bowl, or a plate in a few minutes from a lump of clay. Their workshops were situated with the brick and tile works at the edge of town, not far from a stream. There they had space to store their raw materials and to dry and stock their products. The tanneries were also often located a distance from the built-up area because they emitted bad odors. Nearer to the city center were the blacksmiths and coppersmiths. Then came the carpenters' shops, the weavers, the shoemakers, the tailors and embroiderers, and finally, nearest to the great mosque and the seat of government, were the jewelers and perfumers.

Being both manufacturers and traders, the artisans worked while the clients watched. The spectacle was often fascinating. In the picture a glass blower removes a ball of red-hot glass from the oven at the end of a rod. When he blows through the rod, a vase, flask, or long-necked bottle forms at the other end. On display in the workshop are golden or enameled pieces of superb color and rare technical perfection. It was this colored glass that the Crusaders from Europe would mistake for precious stones!

Procedures, styles, and decorative motifs circulated throughout the empire. The techniques of damascening (Damascus), etching and inlaying objects of iron and steel, such as swords or knives, reached Toledo. The art of decorating leather reached Morocco, where it became very popular. Leather tanning and many other crafts even reached as far as Europe. From the Middle East, Venice imported the techniques, the raw materials, and the secrets of glass making. For centuries the city guarded these secrets jealously, hidden away on the island of Murano.

In this workshop in Old Cairo, master glassmakers are blowing glass. The blowing is performed when the material is incandescent. The objects are decorated with gilt and enamel. The apprentice standing at the left is preparing to blow glass.

This potter is working on a wooden wheel. It has a vertical axis, the ends of which are attached to two horizontal round disks. The clay from which the piece will be "thrown" is placed on the upper disk, while the lower disk is set in motion by the potter's foot.

You could smell the perfumer's quarter from far away! The manufacturers used incense, ambergris, and many flower essences, such as violet, jasmine, rose, and orange blossom. For their clientele, they stocked soaps, creams, depilatory pastes, and henna, a hair dye in powder form.

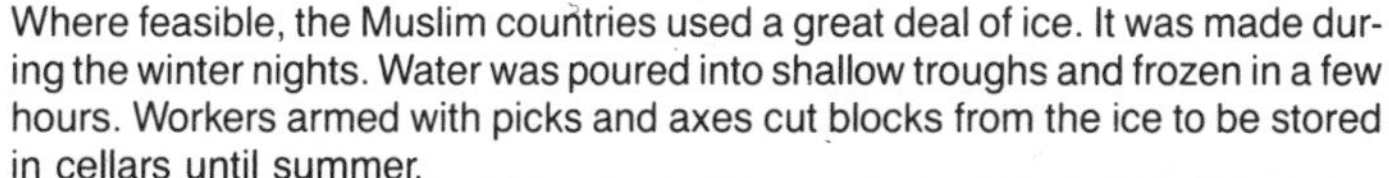

Where feasible, the Muslim countries used a great deal of ice. It was made during the winter nights. Water was poured into shallow troughs and frozen in a few hours. Workers armed with picks and axes cut blocks from the ice to be stored in cellars until summer.

This artisan is decorating the sheath of a saber by encrusting it with slivers of gold. This procedure also makes use of silver and copper wire. In the background an apprentice is shaping gold into wire. The artisans created magnificent designs based on letters or arabesques in the form of flowers.

Skins were soaked in vats for three days and nights and then put into another bath before being tanned. Next came a process that made the leather supple. Finally it would be ready to be made into shoes, or Moroccan leather, or used to bind books.

In the Great Cities

The words *gigantic* and *colossal* are not excessive when used to describe the fifteen or so capital cities that were scattered throughout the Muslim world of the tenth century. At the time it took no less than a day to traverse the nine-mile length of the city of Samarra. Groups of buildings ten stories high in Old Cairo and in Baghdad looked like mountains from a distance. These buildings, usually constructed around a courtyard and a green space, varied in comfort. Some sheltered two hundred people each. Controlling these people caused the supervisors and the owners a great deal of trouble. Some tenants did not hesitate to disappear — with the doors! However, the private home, or *bayt,* was the most common type of dwelling. Its looks changed from one quarter to another and from one city to another, depending on the social level of its inhabitants and the local climate. But each home conformed to a basic model. Whether it was in the populous quarter crisscrossed by a labyrinth of narrow streets and blind alleys, or in the middle of a garden surrounded by walls, the home was always built around a courtyard.

In the richest dwellings the courtyard was embellished by a decorative basin and fountains. All doors and windows opened onto this courtyard. The exterior walls were blank, with no openings.

In the most luxurious homes lived the members of the court and the army, the scribes *(koutab)*, the merchants, the entrepreneurs, and the men of religion, letters, and sciences. Together, they formed the upper layer of society. The businessmen and craftsmen belonged to this same class.

Muslim society also included the masses — the poor, the beggars, and those whose work depended on other people. This social stratum was the cradle of innumerable revolts of a political or religious nature.

Awnings, immense sheets of canvas, were hung between the buildings to protect crowds from the sun's rays. There were no trees. The streets echoed with the sounds of vendors selling their flowers, fruits, vegetables, and carpets. Fortune-tellers could often be found sitting on the ground in the shade, predicting the future by tracing marks in the sand.

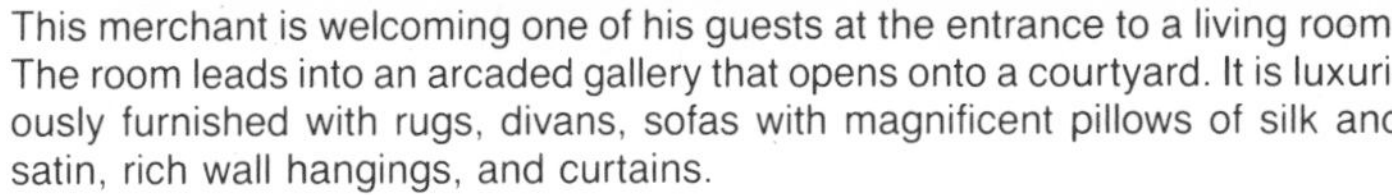

This merchant is welcoming one of his guests at the entrance to a living room. The room leads into an arcaded gallery that opens onto a courtyard. It is luxuriously furnished with rugs, divans, sofas with magnificent pillows of silk and satin, rich wall hangings, and curtains.

In the overpopulated cities, riots by strikers and the poor erupted periodically, marked by scenes of pillage and burning. The riots were caused by shortages and floods but were also sometimes stirred up by political and religious leaders.

Boxes and coffers of sculpted wood, like the chest above, were an essential part of the house and palace furnishings. Sculpted wood, whether inlaid with ivory or not, was used lavishly for doors, dividing walls, and window shutters.

These dockworkers have stopped work to demand a pay raise. Militiamen armed with clubs are confronting them. In Baghdad and Basra, strikes by sailors and dockworkers sometimes occurred. Since the city's food supplies depended on these workers, their strikes brought on a rise in the prices of foodstuffs. To explain their reasons, the strikers would organize meetings in the nearby mosques. In the end the armed police, *al-chourta,* would intervene in a brutal way and force the strikers to go back to work.

Supermarkets and Department Stores

The development of cities led to an increase in consumer spending. Markets, called *suks* or *bazaars,* overflowed with goods from every corner of the world. They were organized by category of product and by artisan's guilds. Small shops of similar size were ranged along both sides of vaulted streets. The streets were long and broad and were sometimes entirely covered. In the case of a luxury bazaar or suk, iron bars closed the entrance gates at night.

The organization of the markets according to specialty inspired competition, which benefited the customers. It also made the task of controlling the markets easier. Agents of the *Sahib as-suk* or *Muhtasib* were responsible for the suk and hunted down shopkeepers who charged fraudulent prices, used short weights, or misrepresented the quality of their goods. The agents were also in charge of public safety and traffic, and they fined those who overloaded their pack animals.

Street hawkers were everywhere. They made their presence known with loud cries describing the excellent quality of their goods or by the tinkling of little bells hung around their animals' collars. The goods they sold ranged from fans, brooms, and rat traps to blocks of ice during the summer months.

In each suk or bazaar there were restaurants, grills, and sherbet shops. Just like the bakers, butchers, millers, dairies, and slaughterhouses, these businesses were under constant surveillance by those who investigated fraud and who controlled public health. Each residential quarter of the city had its own suk or bazaar containing shops of every guild, where all sorts of foodstuffs and other wares could be found. To some extent these were the department stores and supermarkets of a thousand years ago.

In the bazaar or suk of brass and copper workers, the shops were the same size. There were no display windows or doors. The ground floor was raised and the mezzanine was sometimes used as an office. Seated on a cushion or rug facing the street, the artisans worked in front of their customers. Here, the man in the foreground hammers a copper pot while farther back another artisan has just finished chiseling a red copper tray.

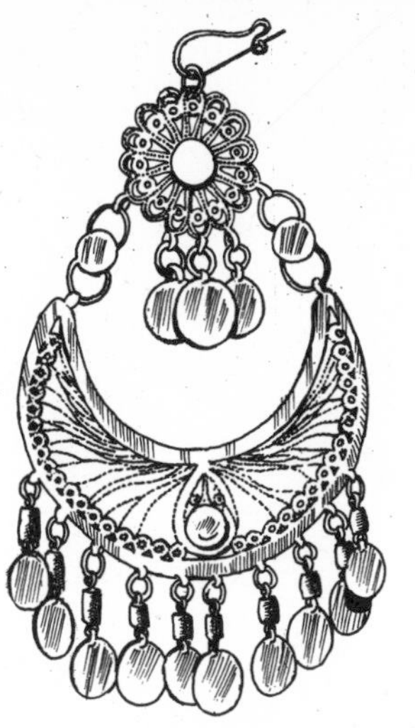

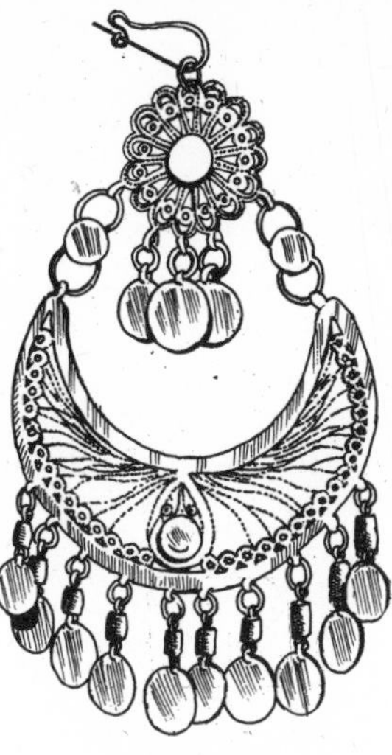

These earrings give an idea of the level of technical and artistic perfection achieved by Muslim artisans. They excelled at producing elegant filigree jewelry made of gold and silver thread intertwined and welded together.

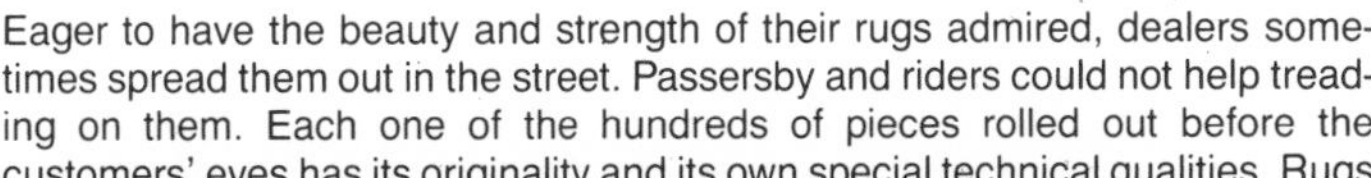

This woman seems to be dreaming as she tries on a sumptuous set of gold jewelry. In the background, another woman is bartering to try to bring down the price of a necklace. Skillful stonecutters furnished the jewelers with precious stones. Crystal was made for the first time at Cordova in the eleventh century.

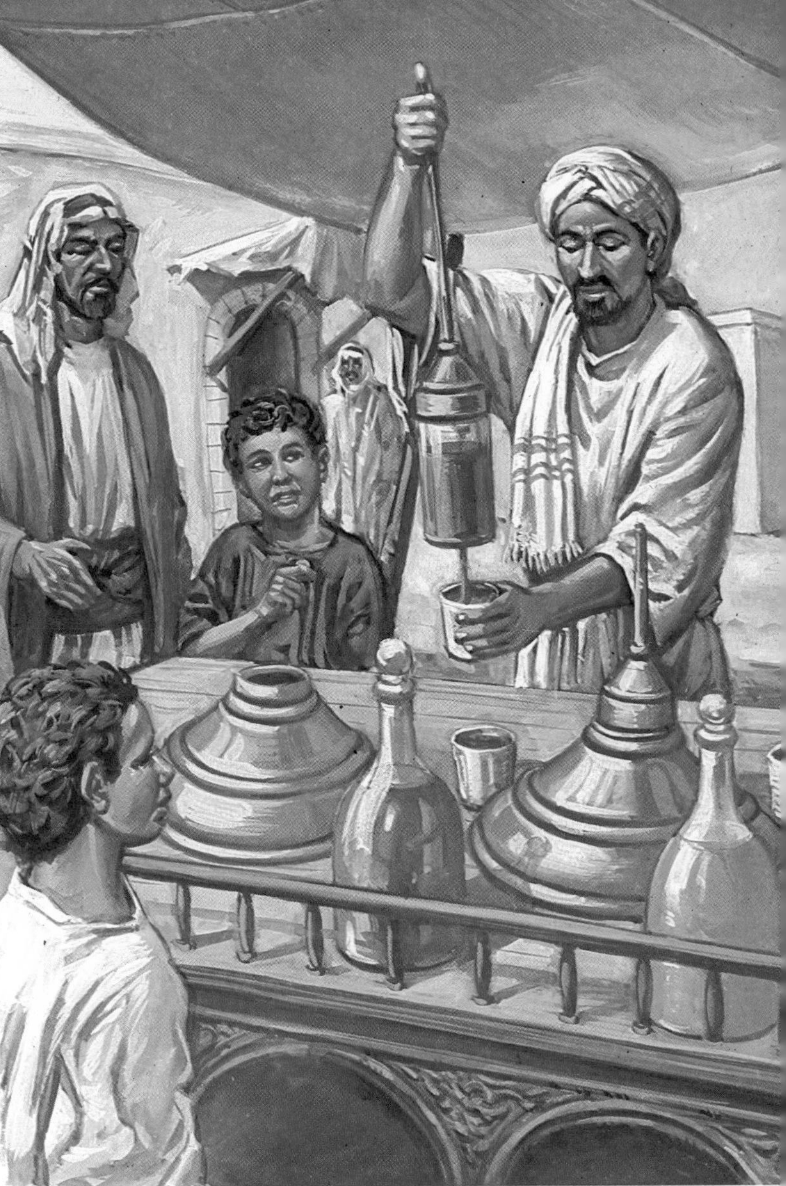

No lively square was without its refreshment seller. On their counters, copper vats with gleaming lids held ices and sherbets. Syrups and fruit juices were kept in large flasks. Jars of water were used to wash the cups.

Eager to have the beauty and strength of their rugs admired, dealers sometimes spread them out in the street. Passersby and riders could not help treading on them. Each one of the hundreds of pieces rolled out before the customers' eyes has its originality and its own special technical qualities. Rugs made in nomads' tents do not in the least resemble those from the village or town workshops. The decorative motifs, the colors, the weave, the embroidery, and the materials used, all differ according to where the rugs were made.

A Multiracial Society

In the Muslim world, Christians, Jews, and members of other religions were allowed to keep their places of worship, their community organizations, and their laws. These groups appointed their own representatives in the government to look after their interests. These minorities took an active part in social life. They practiced nearly every trade — farmer, artisan, banker, trader, doctor. Legally they could not occupy high military or political positions and obviously no religious ones. But certain of them, nevertheless, achieved the post of vizier, a minister of state. Under some monarchs or following grave crises, measures were announced, but usually not applied, against these minorities.

Certain Christians and Jews played the role of intermediary in the enormous traffic in pagan slaves — Slavs from Europe, Turks from Central Asia, and blacks from Africa. Thousands of children were bought as slaves in the markets of the Sudan and of Venice, Kiev, Aachen, and Bulgaria. At Verdun, Prague, and, particularly, in the Christian monasteries of Aswan, boys were subjected to the terrible operation of castration. They could be sold for more money if they were castrated, and they often ended up in the palaces as eunuchs. Transactions with regard to these boys and to pretty young women were conducted in luxurious quarters.

In Muslim cities there were many slaves, but freed slaves — that is, men and women who had become free again — were also to be seen. Muslims considered the freeing of a slave who had converted to Islam to be an act of piety. Thousands of slaves, freed slaves, and concubines lived in the palaces. In certain eras, most of the caliphs were themselves the sons of slaves. Racism was unknown in Islamic society. Intermarriage took place at all social levels. Blacks often governed white populations without anyone refusing to obey them because of the color of their skin.

These women were brought from Nubia, Turkestan, Byzantium, and the Slavic countries to the slave market. To bring the best price they were decked out with jewels and makeup and their hair was dressed. Merchants would praise each woman's special qualities to prospective buyers. Buyers would examine slaves carefully, right down to their teeth, before purchasing them!

In front of the cadi (judge), this slave displays the scars of beatings received from his master. This is sufficient proof for him to gain his liberty. When a woman slave became a concubine, her children were born free. She herself would eventually be freed — at the latest, on the death of her master.

Male slaves were used for all kinds of jobs. They followed the trade of artisans and ran businesses for their masters. Many of them were sent to the army. They made up the main body of the imperial guard and ended up holding much of the real power.

At Jewish festivals the songs, dances, and music were very similar to those of the Muslims. With the Arab conquest, the Jewish community ceased to be persecuted and found prosperity once more. In Spain, Jewish culture lived through a golden age for five centuries.

In Baghdad and Cordova, young female slaves were instructed in music, singing, dancing, and literature in specialized schools like this one. Then they were able to enliven the receptions and parties given by the wealthy and the princes.

When a Marriage Takes Place

For three days, from dawn to dusk, the house has been a beehive of activity. Preparations for the marriage, that very evening, of the eldest son of the family are in full swing. The women move feverishly about. Relatives and neighbors get on with the baking of cakes, making sweetmeats and bread as well as arranging and decorating the rooms and the patio. An identical kind of excitement reigns in the bride's house.

Everywhere in the Muslim world, engagements and marriages followed the same ceremonial pattern almost to the last detail. Generally speaking, the first contacts between the families of the future couple took place at the bathhouse (*hamman*), through the mediation of the women in both families. Then the boy's father would make contact with the girl's, either directly or through an intermediary. The proposal, however, was made solemnly, in the presence of one or two people of consequence. The dowry that the young man had to pay was decided. Usually this was a token or symbolic sum, but it could reach very high figures. The amount was included in the marriage contract drawn up by the cadi, a magistrate who took care to ascertain the mutual consent of the fiancés. In pre-Islamic Arabia, in certain circles of society, the birth of a girl was considered a calamity. Often girl babies would be put to death. Islam abolished this infanticide forever.

The Koran allows a man to have four wives, for polygamy existed in the non-Christian societies of the Near East. Each wife has very precise guarantees and rights in case she is cast out, or if the marriage is dissolved.

The injunctions contained in the Koran on the decency of women's dress have led to their having to wear the veil in certain periods of history.

This bride is led to her husband's house in a litter carried by a camel and richly adorned for the occasion. The musicians play, one on a tambourine hung around his neck and the other on the *zourna,* a kind of oboe. On one side, two men are carrying gifts for the bride.

The ceremony of the *hamman,* a steambath, was part of the preparation for the wedding night. The engaged couple invited his and her best friends. Whether public or private, the hamman always contained several rooms topped by cupolas decorated with stained glass. Near the entrance was a large room for undressing and resting. It led into a succession of rooms that got warmer and warmer, where massages, depilation, hair dressing, and hair dyeing with henna took place.

Cooks, recruited for the occasion, prepared soup, roasts, and stews for dozens of guests. As early as the ninth century, many books discussed the art of combining aromatics and spices in seasoning, the art of cooking, and dietetics.

The bride was sumptuously adorned. Music and song helped celebrate her happiness. Her friends and some of the guests danced in high spirits. Among the happy throng, drinks, pastries, and sweets circulated endlessly.

At nightfall the bridegroom rode on horseback through the streets of the city. He was followed by a long retinue and accompanied by torchbearers and musicians. Multicolored flares, fired like rockets, lit up the sky.

Luxurious Palaces

Protected by an imposing wall, the sovereign's residence, a veritable town within a town, sometimes stretched for almost a mile. It was a political, an administrative, and a military stronghold as well as an artistic and intellectual center. For one reception given for an ambassador, no less than thirty-two thousand silk curtains embroidered with gold and silver, twenty-two thousand rugs, and about a hundred extra divans more would be brought out. Included in one palace was an ornamental basin filled with mercury. Four gilded ships sailed on this silvery pool. In the reception hall of another palace, an artificial tree of gold and silver weighing about 3,300 pounds would rise out of the ground, propelled by a mechanism. On its branches, birds made from precious metals sang while fountains sent up jets of water perfumed with roses and musk. Wild animals, including lions, elephants, and giraffes populated this menagerie.

In the caliph's residence there were discussions between doctors of law, poetry readings, and festivities made merry by singers, dancers, and musicians. The governors, people of distinction, and rich merchants imitated their sovereigns. For example, the favorite wife of the caliph decorated her sandals with precious stones. Her rival began wearing a headband ornamented with stones, meant really to hide a mark on her forehead. Immediately, these two whims became fashionable. Another example of setting fashion comes down to us from the ninth century. Ziryab, a musician and singer from Baghdad, emigrated to Cordova (822–857). His talent and personality turned the city into a beacon of elegance, fashion, and good taste. He was to dictate the habit of wearing different outfits for different seasons, of using glassware instead of gold and silver goblets at table, and, during festivities, of serving dishes in a certain order that is still correct today.

This dancer in the large drawing room of the palace is doing a number with sabers. Another woman is accompanying her on a tambourine framed by little disks that tinkle like bells. On the left a musician is playing the *oud,* a lute with five double chords.

As generations passed, the protocol for an audience before the caliph lost its simplicity. Ostentation and ceremony were used to magnify the caliph's person and, at the same time, to assert his authority. Even an ambassador representing a foreign power had to kiss the ground before him.

Poetry influenced all of society and contributed to the formation of the public taste. Certain great poets used their talents to defend important causes in the face of tyranny. Others preferred adulatory praise, religious subjects, or as with the poet we see here, bacchic verse in praise of wine.

The sovereign, sitting on the highest step of the minbar of the great mosque, is presenting his heir to the members of the community. A dignitary reads the letter in which the old prince willingly gives up his rights.

In one of the many administrative offices, the *kuttab*, or secretaries, dealt with innumerable state documents. They were known for their wide-ranging knowledge, and could be recognized by their elegant clothes, and the cut of their hair in the form of a *V* on their foreheads.

Princely Pastimes

At the beginning of the empire, the caliphs passed their days, which were interrupted by prayers, in receiving civil and military officials. They also listened to plaintiffs who asked for decisions on their cases and to the poor who pleaded for assistance. The caliphs, along with their subordinates, handled every type of problem and managed the finances of the empire. As the empire grew, the administrative organization became increasingly burdensome. Little by little, the caliphs, sometimes unwillingly, turned over power to governors, generals, emirs, and viziers. The caliphs then had more time for their own amusements.

Large-scale hunts were prepared by masters of the hunt assisted by huntsmen, guards, and all kinds of servants. During these hunts the members of the royal party could flaunt their luxurious life-styles. Apart from the physical exercise and the relaxation it gave them, the caliphs took advantage of these occasions to display their vigor and to reveal their skill and courage in facing savage beasts and killing those that were harmful. The capture of wild animals helped to stock the zoos.

In the hippodrome *(or maydan)* near the palace, it was common for the sovereign to participate in horse racing. The caliphs played polo and took part in acrobatics and riding exercises. With their associates they enjoyed chess, backgammon, dice games, conversation with learned men on chosen subjects, readings of poetry, and performances by jugglers.

Fetes, banquets, and sumptuous parties were held inside the royal palaces. They took place amid extraordinary luxury: lights illuminated the gardens, with their fountains and canals; delicate scents emanated from incense burners; flowers were spread around the area or handed to the revelers; many delicious foods and fine wines were served in abundance; and a great number of the very best dancers and musicians provided entertainment. Everything was dazzling.

Deer were captured with lasso. The rope was tied to the horse's collar, enabling the hunter to control the operation and to avoid strangling the beast. Animals caught in such a manner often ended their days in the palace's zoological park.

The prince loved to play polo with his friends and nobles in the hippodrome near the palace. This sport was favored throughout the empire, including Muslim Spain. The matches were usually followed by splendid banquets.

The gardens of royal residences often had menageries. Sometimes they were actually immense zoological parks open to the public on certain days. Many canals crisscrossed the habitats occupied by all sorts of rare animals. The Samarra Zoo in Mesopotamia covered about twenty square miles.

Combat between rams, like cock fighting, was a spectacle that could be seen on street corners and in the squares. Two rams would dash at one another from a distance and crash together, horns against horns, time and again until one of them was exhausted. People would watch these duels with passionate interest. Some spectators would wager on the outcome, even though betting was strictly forbidden. It was common for the combat to be followed by a brawl over bets.

The People's Festivals

For one month each year, after sundown and until late at night, the towns and villages took on a festive air. This happened during the month-long celebration of *Ramadan*. All through the day, every healthy adult Muslim abstained from food and drink. But in the evening the streets were illuminated and became animated. The bazaars and boutiques opened up. Many of the faithful took part in vigils in the mosques.

The end of the month was marked by three days of celebration. This was called *Id al-Fitr*, or "the festival of breaking the fast." Men, women, and children appeared in their best clothing. On the first day, after a solemn prayer at the mosque in the morning, the people congratulated each other. At home, cakes especially prepared for the occasion during the final two days of Ramadan were eaten.

The second festival, which took place before the celebration of the birth of the Prophet Muhammad, was that of the sacrifice, *Id al-Adha*. On this day, well-to-do families killed a sheep in memory of the test imposed by God on Abraham. It was at this time that the pilgrimage to Mecca ended. Solidarity with the poor was expressed by the distribution of at least half of the sacrificial animal. The offerings also included sugar candy and cake. Around the mosque, in the squares and the streets, exhibitions by tightrope walkers, animal trainers, and sword swallowers were a big attraction.

Military parades marked the start of a ruler's official journey, or the army's departure for war. Both took place to the rhythm of drums and trumpets. A large crowd would usually gather along the route to admire the uniforms of the cavalry, the discipline of the infantry, and the army's siege machines.

Bear trainers and snake charmers could be found performing for the crowd. Both would profit from the nearness of a market selling grain, fruits, and vegetables outside the ramparts of the city. Peddlers of candies and water would also do a good business.

In the square in front of the mosque, a tightrope walker walks across his cord, making the onlookers breathless with excitement. Drum rolls and the blare of trumpets mark the different phases of this spectacle. When the acrobat finishes a dangerous maneuver, the crowd cheers.

During the last evening of the month of Ramadan, the mosques, markets, and streets were illuminated even more brightly than usual. Spectacular fireworks were added to the light of kerosene and oil lamps. This woman watches the spectacle from her balcony.

On the second day of the *Id al-Fitr* and the *Id al-Adha,* women honored the memory of the dead by visiting their tombs. Along the route to the cemetery, which was usually situated outside the city, young men lined the route in the hope of being favored with a smile.

Al-Mawlid or *Mulud* was the anniversary of the birth of the Prophet Muhammad. The holiday was celebrated with colorful festivities. Brilliant military festivals, which included the cavalry carrying torches, drew large crowds. In some towns, huge decorated arches of triumph were raised for the occasion. The arrival of the Crusaders in the twelfth century put an end to the Muslim's tolerant attitude towards Christians. Until then, though, the Christian festivals of Christmas and Easter as well as celebrations of New Year were held in all the large cities of the Muslim world.

Sports and Games

In about the year 800, the best chess and backgammon players in the empire received pensions from the caliph. Since he was also a great lover of sports, he encouraged them by planning the construction of stadiums and hippodromes and by offering prizes to the champions.

Horse races always attracted a considerable sized crowd eager to bet — even though betting was forbidden by the Koran. Competitions in archery, swimming, fencing, and hurling the javelin attracted many rivals, who competed enthusiastically for the prizes awarded to the victors. Polo and hunting were aristocratic pastimes. The same was true of a ball game played with wooden rackets, an ancestor of modern tennis.

Wrestling was very popular. The matches took place in a covered enclosure that had seats in tiers which could hold thousands of spectators. The feeling of the crowd, animated to begin with, frequently became delirious when a victor pinned the shoulders of his adversary to the mat. Champions often achieved national and international fame. In this way they added to their glory and made their fortunes.

The townspeople, like people in the country, hunted all sorts of wild game in a variety of ways. They used blow pipes, bows and arrows, crossbows, nets, traps, and lassos, as well as greyhounds, gazelle hounds, sparrow hawks, and falcons. Naturally, the animals that were hunted differed from region to region. Bears, lions, tigers, stags, wild boars, wild sheep, and fallow deer were found in mountains and forests. Gazelles, antelopes, ostriches, and many kinds of wild game of fur and feather, lived on the steppes in the desertlike zones.

The hippodrome in Samarra, the Abbasid capital of Iraq, had a superb oval racetrack that measured six and a half miles in circumference. The atmosphere was solemn on the official platform. The governor presided from a seat higher than the rest. Many riders rode without stirrups!

In summer, rich families took vacations to escape the heat and the noise of the cities. Often, they went camping. Loading their pack animals with tents, provisions, and many other indispensable items, they would leave for the country or the mountains.

Wrestlers began their matches by saluting one another and ended by embracing. Many covered rooms, such as this one, existed in the towns. They served as gymnasiums. From morning until evening, young men — amateur or professional athletes — practiced various sports there.

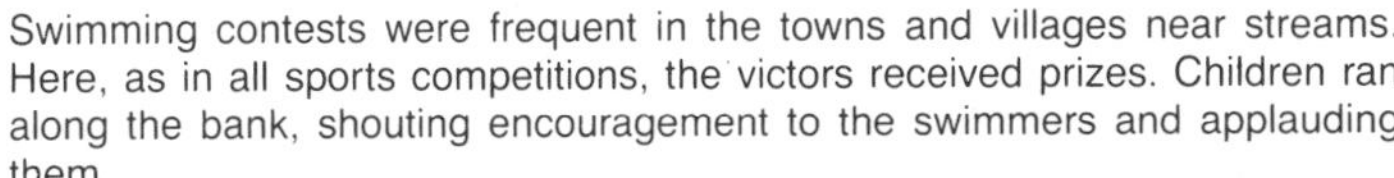

Swimming contests were frequent in the towns and villages near streams. Here, as in all sports competitions, the victors received prizes. Children ran along the bank, shouting encouragement to the swimmers and applauding them.

At the sound of a drum, birds rose from the reeds and flew off. At the same moment, the hunters released falcons or sparrow hawks. Hunting with birds of prey was such a passion with some men that books were written on the art of hawking and falconry.

In stadiums reserved for archery, pumpkins were perched atop poles as a target for archery competitions. The bow and arrow was one of the principal weapons of the Muslim armies. Books on armaments explain the gradual development of the bow and arrow.

Doctors, Surgeons, and Druggists

During the ninth century there were hospitals in all the large towns of the Muslim world. Often housed in palatial buildings, these hospitals were supplied with everything needed. They had many wards and rooms with comfortable beds. Patients with communicable diseases were isolated, as were patients who had been through surgical operations.

The administration kept registers listing the names of the sick who were hospitalized, the care they received, the food they ate, and the cost of everything. Some hospitals even contained a medical library and a school of medicine. At Baghdad in 931, when a diploma, or *ijâza,* was first introduced for the exercise of the profession of medicine, more than 880 candidates applied for it.

In the hospitals, the prisons, and the asylums for the insane, doctors visited their patients every morning. In the charitable institutions these visits took place only twice a week. Doctors traveled through the countryside, giving advice and dispensing remedies. In about the year 1000, mobile clinics appeared. The pharmacies appeared with the opening of the first school of pharmacy.

Due to the work of many scientists, teaching and research on health made great progress. At the end of the ninth century, Razi (known to the Latins as Rhazes) edited an encyclopedia and conducted studies of contagious illnesses, such as measles and smallpox, and of allergies. Among the latter, he analyzed what would be called hay fever nine centuries later. Through the centuries many works, translated into Latin, became essential sources of medical teaching in the Christian West.

In pharmacy laboratories, druggists prepared potions according to directions found in the *Treatise on Medicinal Drugs* by Biruni. In the picture above, the sheets of paper to the left of the window record directions to prepare other remedies. The bulge of the large retort is protected from the fire by a covering of clay.

This dentist is fitting false teeth made of bone into a patient's mouth. Many books on dental care recommended this technique. These books also described the instruments that were necessary for pulling teeth.

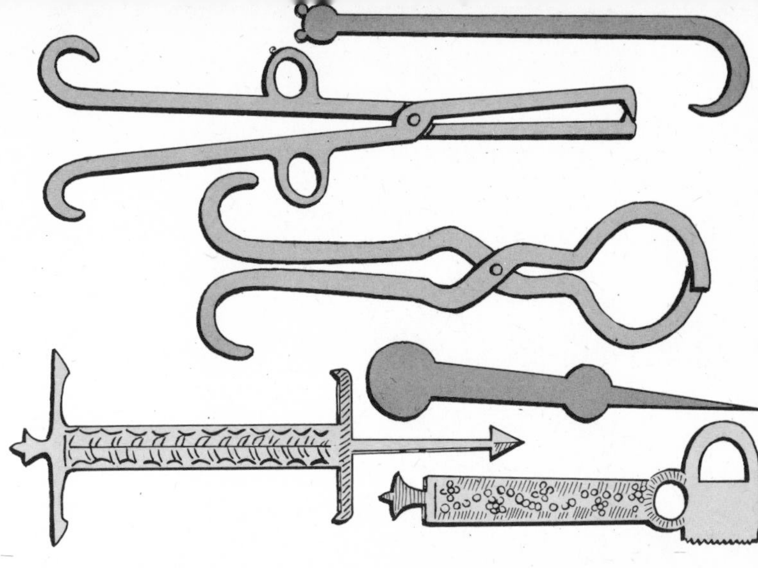

The surgeon Abul Kasem, known in the West as Abulcasis, of Cordova left at his death in 1013 an enormous encyclopedia of thirty volumes. In it he covered, in particular, the different uses of the lancet and surgical operations. He sketched more than two hundred instruments that he had invented.

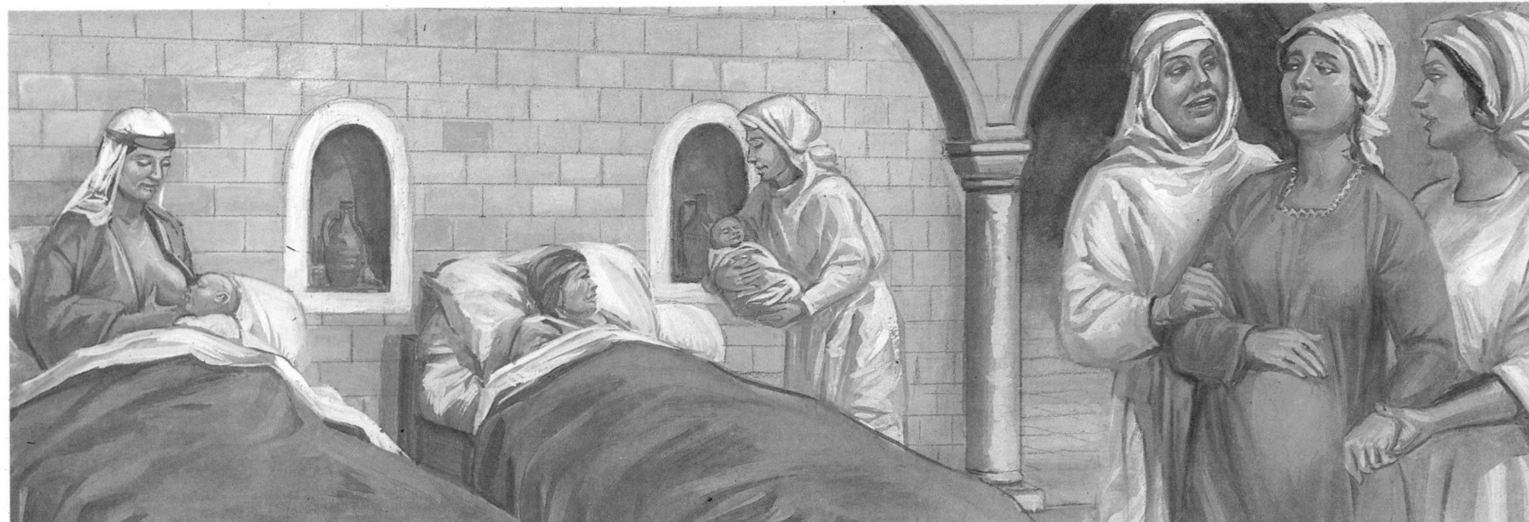

This hospital of a hundred beds was exclusively for women. The doctors and the personnel responsible for the patients were also women. In towns with only one hospital, separate areas were reserved for female patients. To make childbirth, easier, doctors taught a patient the position she should adopt. Surgeons used instruments developed for their specialties. Hospital stays and all medical care were free.

This baker has not obeyed the rules of the sanitary code fixed to the wall. Empty sacks of grain were to be cleaned and suspended out of the reach of rats. To ensure respect for public hygiene, the police made frequent visits to the food stores.

Arabic medicine developed largely on the basis of the work of Greek scientists. Thus inspired by the research of Galen, the book of the *Ten Treatises on the Eye* by Hunayn ibn-Ishaq (ninth century) is precise in its study of anatomy and remained an authority on the subject until the thirteenth century.

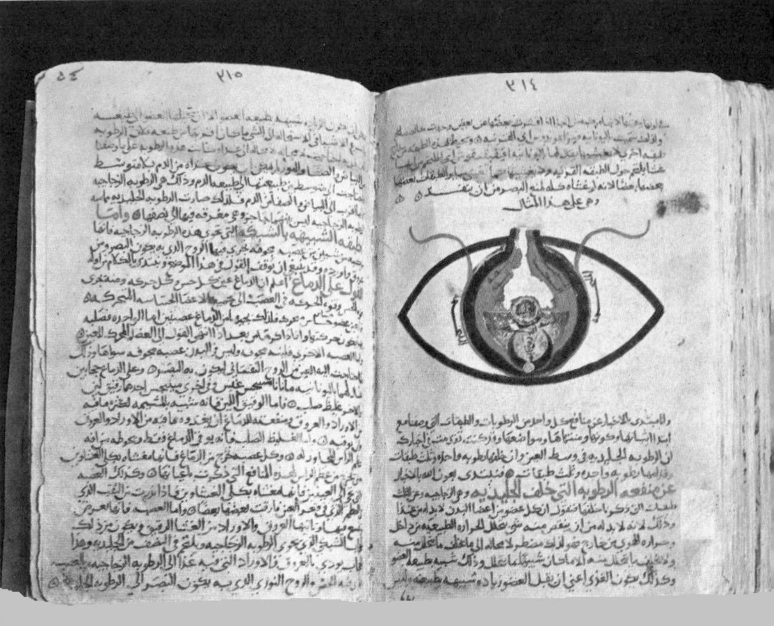

Libraries and Bookstores

At Samarkand in the middle of the eighth century, Chinese prisoners revealed the secret of making paper. It wasn't long before the first paper factories opened in Baghdad. Knowledge of the technique spread and soon arrived in Spain and in Muslim Sicily. But from there it did not reach Italy, France, or the rest of Europe until the thirteenth century.

In all the towns of the Muslim world, bazaars were established with areas where books were produced and sold. In each "publishing house" there was a workshop for copyists who were sometimes women. To earn their livelihood, the copyists labored to reproduce manuscripts faithfully. Their salaries varied according to their knowledge, their handwriting, and their diligence. The price of a book depended on the quality of the work. The book trade was very active and included a number of impressive works. Some specialists traveled from town to town looking for new texts to publish. Others sold only rare books for collectors. In Cordova, nearly everyone knew how to read and write. In Baghdad, intellectuals made up about a third of the population.

Each town had one or more public libraries. Some of these libraries held hundreds of thousands of books. The finest, the Cairo library, contained 1.6 million books. Located in the palace, it was divided into departments according to the different subjects. The volumes were arranged in pigeonholes, one above the other, and were sometimes enclosed in cupboards with lists of titles attached to the doors. Readers used catalogues to locate the books. To borrow the books all they needed to do was give their names and addresses. Some people even had libraries in their homes.

In the foreground, catalogues have been placed in compartments accessible to the public. The globe of the heavens is made of copper, and the map of the world hanging on the wall is silk. In 1005 the most important library in the city was opened in the great palace of Old Cairo. It contained forty rooms.The catalogue of the library in Cordova amounted to forty-four volumes.

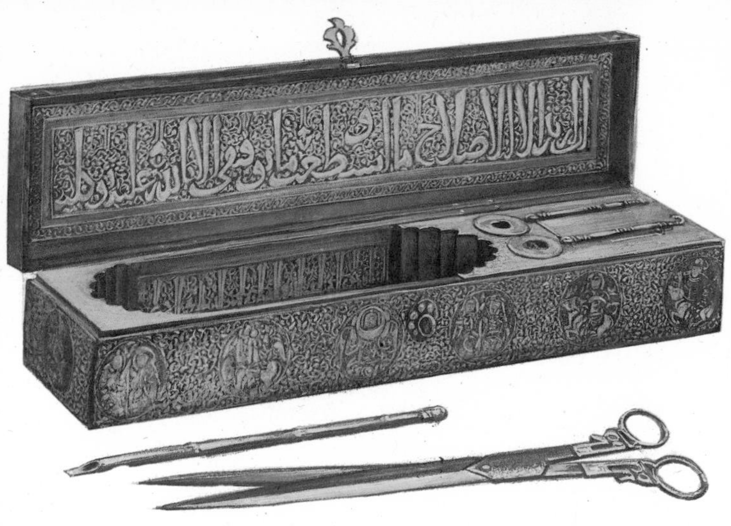

A pen called a *kalam,* was made of a reed or of bamboo sharpened to a point or a blade. The kalam along with the ink and the writing stand, were the principal tools of copyists, calligraphers, scribes, and secretaries. This luxurious writing stand with two ink wells is made of brass with copper and silver decorations.

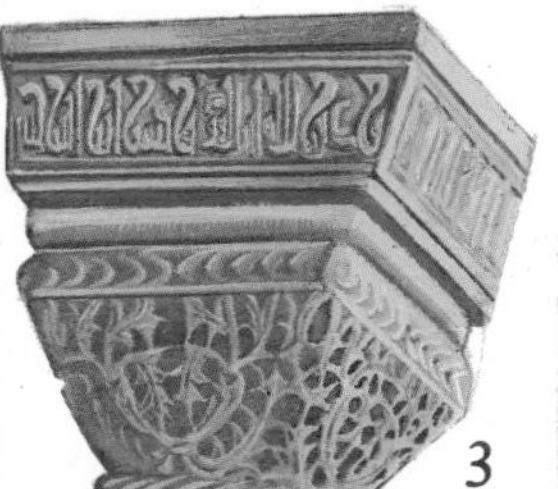

Arabic writing gave birth to the art of calligraphy. Calligraphy was first used in the composition of splendid manuscripts enriched with artistic decoration. Then it was used to decorate other objects and monuments: (1) silver coin; (2) molding in plaster; (3) marble capital; (4) wooden fragment.

Paper pulp was obtained from rags of linen, hemp, and cotton placed with a quantity of water in a vat equipped with four mauls that were moved by a waterwheel. The milky and fibrous substance obtained in this way was fashioned into sheets manually with the aid of a mold, a wooden frame with a fine sieve at the bottom.

In the thirteenth century the atmosphere of liberty and tolerance evaporated. Giving way to fanatical religious movements, some governments gave orders for books to be destroyed. Notably, books on philosophy were burned. But the worst damage was done in Baghdad by the Mongols in 1258. After killing 24,000 learned men, the victors dumped the contents of entire libraries into the river. They burned the rest of the books.

Science and Technology: Tradition and Innovation

"Look for knowledge, even as far as China," said the Prophet Muhammad. Therefore, learning and the spreading of knowledge became a pious undertaking. Official missions, as well as private individuals, traveled the world over in search of new manuscripts, which were immediately translated and copied.

Initially, basic education was provided at the mosques and was limited to reading, writing, and the study of the Koran. For other subjects and for study on higher levels private study groups were formed. Motivated students traveled in pursuit of knowledge from one teacher to another. Only gradually did the state take an interest in education. In the tenth century, the Fatimids founded the first university in Cairo (al-Azhar), and soon a type of religious college, the *madrasa*, began to spread through the Islamic world. In the ninth century, an Abbasid caliph endowed a kind of research institution, the House of Wisdom, where important works of Greek science were translated into Arabic.

The development of arithmetic, geometry, and algebra (from Arabic *al-jabr*) helped with the complicated calculation of taxes, duties, and inheritance rights. It permitted the solution of mechanical problems regarding mills and waterwheels and the construction of all kinds of automated mechanisms as well as toys. These developments were aided by the use of zero and the "Arabic" numerals (which actually came from India) that we use today in place of Roman numerals, which were inconvenient except in the simplest calculations. Scientists also drew up maps and navigation tables, and perfected astronomical instruments to determine the direction of Mecca, the hours of prayer, the month for fasting, and the routes of caravans and ships. In China, Muslim navigators learned to use the magnetic needle, the future compass. For the first time in the Mediterranean region, the triangular sail that we call a lateen was used.

These astronomers are verifying facts concerning the movement of the moon and the planets. They frequently use the term *al-somut*, which became the term *azimuth* in English.

This craftsman is making a portable astrolabe. He is a specialist in the design of measuring and precision instruments, which includes scales of different sizes, clocks, and other automatic mechanisms. Some of these objects were truly works of art.

Al asturlab, the astrolabe, was made of brass or copper. It could be spherical or flat. It consisted of a base with a hole in the middle and two superimposed disks with graduations marked along the edge. It served, in particular, to measure the position of the stars above the horizon and to determine the hour.

The aristocrats had a special liking for automated mechanisms. This nobleman owns an automatic wash basin. The water pours from an ewer held by a statue representing a servant. When "her" master has finished washing, "she" extends the other hand, which holds a towel and a comb.

Students of astronomy, like other students, acquired their knowledge by going from teacher to teacher and from city to city. Their aim was to learn everything they possibly could. They were therefore interested in other subjects, such as mathematics, physics, geography, theology, history, and poetry.

Elementary instruction was given in the schools to all children over seven years of age. They learned writing, the Koran, arithmetic, grammar, spelling, and history. The youngest students used tablets of wood or metal, while the other students used paper notebooks.

The Arabic Language and Script

by Dr. George Krotkoff
Department of Near Eastern Studies, The Johns Hopkins University

The Arabic language is a Semitic language and thus a relative of such languages as Phoenician, Hebrew, Aramaic, Babylonian, and Assyrian. It is the Phoenicians who are normally credited with the invention of the alphabet, i.e. a way of writing in which single speech sounds are represented by special symbols. This is the most economical way of writing, as opposed to such systems where special symbols must be memorized for syllables or whole words. The Phoenician script was further developed by the Arameans and the Hebrews, and already before Islam the Arabs had begun to write their language in a variant of the Aramaic script which was characterized by its cursive lines and the tendency of the letters to connect within one word.

As a result of the Arab conquests both the religion of Islam and the Arabic language were carried to other peoples outside Arabia. Not all people, however, who converted to Islam adopted the Arabic language. Thus, the inhabitants of Mesopotamia, Syria, Egypt, and the rest of North Africa were both Islamized and Arabized, and today they consider themselves part of the Arab nation. In contrast, the Persians, Turks, Malays, and many other peoples of Asia and Africa were Islamized but not Arabized, and retain their respective national identities.

Because Muslims believe that their Scripture, the Koran, is a copy of a heavenly book containing the Divine Word, the script, and with it the art of writing, command a particular respect in the world of Islam. This explains two important facts. On the one hand, all peoples who converted to Islam, but did not adopt Arabic, began to write their own languages with the Arabic script. Only in the course of the twentieth century was the Arabic script replaced by the Roman for such languages as Turkish, Malay, and Swahili, and by the Cyrillic for languages spoken inside the Soviet Union.

Mihrab (prayer niche) of the Great Mosque in Cordova (Spain). The many fields of the design are filled with arabesques, and at the top one can see three lines in guilded Kufi script.

Oronoz Ziolo

â	ا	alif	b	ب	bâ	t	ت	tâ	th	ث	thâ	j	ج	jîm
ḥ	ح	ḥâ	kh	خ	khâ	d	د	dâl	dh	ذ	âl	r	ر	râ
z	ز	zâ	s	س	sîn	sh	ش	shîn	ṣ	ص	âd	ḍ	ض	ḍâd
ṭ	ط	ṭâ	ẓ	ظ	ẓâ	ʿ	ع	ʿayn	gh	غ	ghayn	f	ف	fâ
q	ق	qâf	k	ك	kâf	l	ل	lâm	m	م	mîm	n	ن	nûn
h	ه	hâ	w,û	و	wâw	y,î	ي	yâ						

On the other hand, the respect for writing was reinforced by the prohibition of pictures of living beings in the religious sphere, and this led to the cultivation of calligraphy and the development of beautiful writing as a vehicle for the Divine Word and as the main decoration on all spaces inside and outside of religious buildings, such as mosques, madrasas, and tombs. Two main styles of writing evolved: the elegant curvilinear Naskhi, and the heavier monumental, angular Kufi.

The Arabic Alphabet

The Arabic alphabet consists of twenty eight letters which are written from right to left. Since the symbols inherited from the Aramaic alphabet were not sufficient to express all sounds of the Arabic language, some letters had to do double duty and their different functions were differentiated by means of additional dots placed above or below the body of the letter (see the table on this page). Some sounds of the Arabic language are quite different from those of English. Therefore, certain conventions have been adopted by scholars in order to express them through Roman characters or other symbols (ʾ for a hiatus separating two vowels, ʿ for a crackling sound in the throat, a dot under an *ḥ* for a very sharp, hissing *ḥ*, etc.).

There are no special characters for vowels. Normally, short vowels are not written at all, while the three letters ا و ى are also used to express the long vowels *â*, *î*, *û* (the distinction between short and long is very important in Arabic). Someone who knows Arabic will know from the context how to pronounce a given word, just as the user of an American telephone directory recognizes *lwyr* for lawyer. For purposes of learning, however, and for the avoidance of ambiguity in the holy text of the Koran, special signs (little slanting lines, commas, circles, etc.) were invented in order to mark all the details of the pronunciation precisely. An example of such a "vocalized" text can be seen in the sample from a Koran manuscript shown at the top of the next page.

Detail of the minaret of Jâm (Afghanistan) with its inscription in blue glazed brick.

Rapho/Michaud

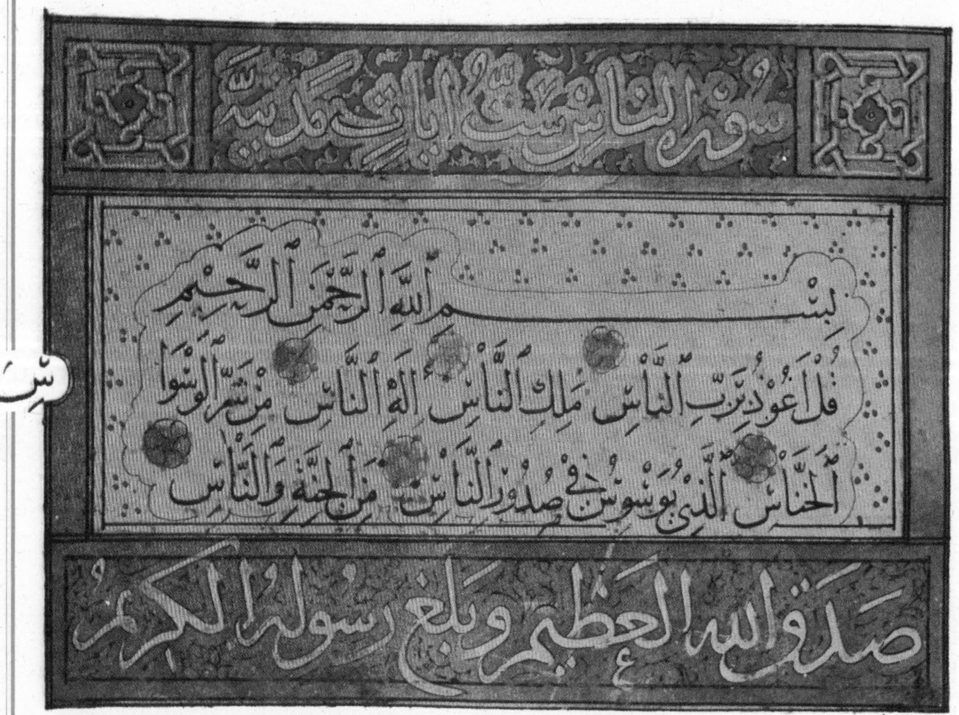

Ornament from an illuminated manuscript.

Page from an ornate Koran manuscript in Naskhi script.

In the alphabetic table, the letters are shown in their isolated, i.e., unconnected form, with the sound value on the left and the name of the letter on the right. Only the six letters و ز ر ذ د ا cannot be connected to a following letter and thus do not change in the context of a word. If a word is formed using them, there will be spaces between the letters: دار *dâr* = "house". All the other letters must be connected to a following letter within a word, which necessitates certain adjustments of their shapes and loss of the curved parts below the line of writing. Thus, to write the word *jabal* "mountain" we need the three letters (from right to left!) ل + ب + ج , but the complete word will look like this: جبل ; *jalasa* "to sit": س + ل + ج = جلس .

A few vocalized examples: وَزِيرٌ *wazîrun* = "a vizier" (the ending *un*, expressed by means of two signs for *u*, has the function of an indefinite article: صِفْرٌ *sifrun* "a zero"; لِسَانٌ *lisânun* = "a tongue"; اَلسَّلَامُ عَلَيْكُمْ . *assalâmu ʿalaykum* = "peace be upon you" (the three-pronged sign over the *s* means "double the letter" because the preceding *l* of the definite article *al* is assimilated to it).

The Arabic Numbers

Although we call our usual number symbols Arabic numbers, they are not the same as those used by Arabs today. Some are similar enough to be recognized, but others are not. The differences are, of course, due to the borrowing between two cultures with different writing habits, and to centuries of separate evolution. The Arabs, in turn, learned these numbers from India, where the zero was invented, and therefore call them Indian numbers. Here is a comparison of the two series:

1 2 3 4 5 6 7 8 9 0
١ ٢ ٣ ٤ ٥ ٦ ٧ ٨ ٩ ٠

A plate from Nishapur (NW Iran, 10th c.) with a decorative inscription in Kufi script.

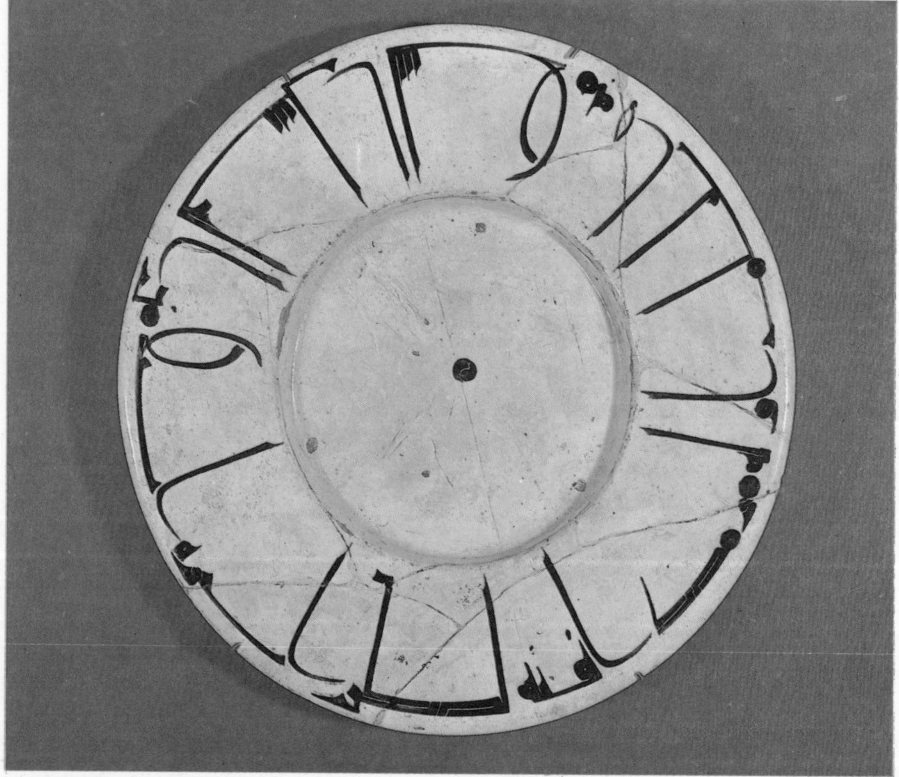

Lauros/Giraudon

The Distant Origin of La Fontaine's Fables

As Jean de La Fontaine, the famous French writer of fables, himself acknowledged, one of his sources of inspiration was a collection of stories and fables of Indo-Iranian origin. They had been passed on to the West thanks to an expanded eighth-century Arabic translation. This work was called the *The Book of Kalila and Dimna*, or the *Fables of Bidpai* from the name of the philosopher who wrote it for an Indian king sometime in the fourth century, but in India it was known as the *Panchatantra*. It had reached Persia in the sixth century; two centuries later, the Persian convert to Islam, Ibn al-Muqaffa, translated it from Pahlavi, the language of the Persian court, into Arabic. As so often happens, the translator and his successors not only translated the work, but also added to it.

From the first Arabic version in prose, a poetic version, and then translations into other languages were made. We know a Greek translation from the eleventh century, a Hebrew one from the twelfth, and a Latin one from the second half of the thirteenth. After that, the book became well known even as far away as Spain. The Latin version which inspired La Fontaine seems to have been translated from the Greek.

Kalila and Dimna, which was first intended as a book of wisdom and advice for kings, was to become a popular work within the reach of everyone, regardless of country or language. By having animals speak like humans and giving them human feelings, qualities, and vices, the author was able to express himself more freely.

Throughout The Book of Kalila and Dimna, Bidpai, the prince of philosophers, answers questions put by the king on friendship, sincerity, trust, deception, hatred, injustice, and every manner of behavior displayed by human beings toward each other. The answers come in the form of a succession of stories and little fables, each illustrating an idea.

The first chapter, for instance, deals with a friendship between two individuals that is transformed into hatred because of the treachery of a third. This third is the jackal called Dimna, Kalila's brother. Both brothers are knowledgeable and clever, but Dimna is driven by ambition and arrogance. When they are appointed keepers of the gate by their king (the lion), Dimna, discontented with this lot, decides that his place

The hare and the elephant at the spring.

is in the king's inner circle as his counselor. And he succeeds in getting there. But Dimna is fiercely jealous of the king's friendship with the ox, so he convinces the lion that his companion is plotting against him and means to injure him. As a result of this the ox is finally executed.

Ibn al-Muqaffa, desiring that truth should triumph and wickedness be punished, added to the tale a chapter on Dimna's trial, which ends in his death.

Through the chapters of the book passes a parade of well-known animals, in particular the monkey, the crow, the vulture, the duck, the lobster, the camel, the louse, and the flea. In their relationships with humans, the most intelligent animals, thanks to their good sense and cooperation, succeed in getting themselves out of exceedingly difficult situations. More than once, hunters come home empty-handed, shamefaced, and furious. But when the animals are among themselves, the weakest sometimes succeed in making fun of the strongest. The following tale, called "The Hare and the Elephant" is one example among many.

The fox and the drum.

The lion killing the ox, in front of Kalila and Dimna.

The Hare and The Elephant

The story goes that some elephants, overwhelmed by a terrible thirst caused by a drought that had been ravaging their region for years, complained to their king. The king dispatched prospectors in all directions, with orders to find a spring. One of them discovered a very copious spring called the Spring of the Moon. Followed by his subjects, the king made his way there to quench his thirst.

The spring was in an area inhabited by hares. The elephants stamped on them, even getting some in their holes. Those who escaped banded together and went to see their king. "You know what a massacre the elephants have perpetrated," they said to him. "The next time they come to drink, they might exterminate the rest of us. You must find some way to save us."

"All who wish to do so may offer their advice," said the king. Firouz, a hare favored by the king because of his knowledge and cunning, came forward and said, "I propose that the king send me to speak to the elephants. He can send with me someone he trusts, who will report to him all that I say and do."

"I have complete faith in you," answered the king. "Go to the elephants and tell them what you like, speaking on my behalf. Be aware, however, that it is through the diplomacy of the emissary that the value and qualities of the one who has sent him are judged. Be flexible and conciliatory, for a messenger can by his remarks either pacify the temper of others or unleash it."

Firouz left on a night of a full moon for the territory of the elephants. There, so as not to be trampled upon, he climbed to the top of a hill. He called the king of the elephants by name and said to him: "It is the moon that has sent me to you. And since a messenger can only fulfill his mission, he is not to blame, even if what he has to report is hard to accept."

"And what is your message?" asked the king of the elephants.

"The moon says to you: When a powerful being, sure of his strength in the face of weakness, allows himself to be blinded to the point of defying those more powerful than himself, he risks the worst misfortune and even, death itself. Because you are sure of your strength with smaller animals, you dare to defy me by coming, with your subjects, to drink and to trouble the spring that bears my name. I warn you. Don't do it again, or I will cause you to lose your sight and your life, too. If you do not believe my message, come immediately to the spring. I will meet you there."

Taken aback by Firouz's words, the king of the elephants followed him to the spring. There, as he looked at the surface of the water, he saw the moon's reflection.

"Take some water with your trunk," Firouz said to him. "Wash your face with it, and prostrate yourself before the moon."

The elephant did as he was told. But as soon as he plunged his trunk into the spring, the water became agitated and seemed to come to life in the moonlight. "What is the matter with the moon," asked the elephant, "that it is so excited? Do you think it's angry because I enjoy its water?"

"That's exactly it," replied Firouz. "Come on. Prostrate yourself."

And the elephant knelt down, apologized, and promised that he and his companions would never again return to the spring.

The lion listening to his mother.

The crow, the turtle, the rat, and the gazelle.

GLOSSARY

Alchemy A combination of science and magic that was studied to find a method to produce gold and silver from cheaper metals.
Allah God
Alms Money or gifts given to help the poor.
Astrolabe A navigational instrument used to determine the position of the sun and other stars in relation to a given point.
Azimuth A line of longitude in the sky or heavens.

Bedouins Wandering Arabs who live in the desert.

Caliph The head of the Muslim state.
Caravan A group of people and pack animals traveling together, frequently across a desert.
Caravanseries The inns which were built around a central courtyard where caravans stopped on their journeys.
Cartography The study or making of maps and charts.
Casbah A section in some North African cities with winding, mazelike streets.
Copyists Those who made written copies of manuscripts.
Crusades The military expeditions of the eleventh, twelfth, and thirteenth centuries organized by European Christians with the purpose of taking the Holy Land back from the Muslims. Those who took part in a Crusade were called *Crusaders.*

Damascene A technique of decorating metal with wavy inlaid or etched patterns.

Fable A story that is meant to teach a lesson.
Five Pillars of Islam *Hajj, Salat, Shahadah, Sawm,* and *Zakat* (see individual entries).

Hajj The pilgrimage to Mecca. The fifth pillar of Islam.
Hegira Muhammad's departure for Mecca. When translated from Arabic it literally means flight, or emigration.

Imam An Islamic prayer leader.
Irrigation To bring water to dry land through pipes, ditches, or streams.
Islam Submission to God.

Ka'aba The central shrine of Islam, located in Mecca.
Koran The book of God.
Kufic characters The letters of the Arabic alphabet that were used in writing copies of the Koran.

Maghreb North Africa.
Mihrab The recess in the wall of the prayer hall of a mosque that indicates the direction to face during prayer.
Minaret A tall tower of a mosque from where the muezzin calls the people to prayer.
Monotheistic Belief in only one god.
Mosque An Islamic place of worship.
Muezzin The crier who calls the people to prayer.
Muslim One who submits.

Nomad A member of a wandering tribe that moves from one place to another in search of food, grazing land for livestock, etc.

Oasis A fertile green area in the middle of a desert.

Pilgrimage A journey made to a holy place, Mecca for example.
Polytheism Belief in more than one god.
Prophet One who preaches what has been revealed to him.

Qadi A judge.
Qanat A canal built for irrigation.

Ramadan The ninth month of the Islamic calendar.
Ribat A fort or fortress built on the Muslim frontier.

Salat A ritual prayer, said five times a day. The second pillar of Islam.
Sawm A fast. The fourth pillar of Islam.
Schism The division of a religion into opposing groups.
Shahadah The profession of faith (". . . there is no other god but Allah, and Muhammad is his messenger"). The first pillar of Islam.
Souk A bazaar or market.

Vizier A high officer in the Muslim Government.

Zakat Alms, tax. The third pillar of Islam.

INDEX